DEDALUS IRISH POETS

AN ANTHOLOGY

The Dedalus Press
24 The Heath, Cypress Downs, Dublin 6W, Ireland

Cover design by Niamh Foran based on an
original sculpture by John Behan.

ISBN 1 873790 10 4

The Dedalus Press acknowledges the assistance of
An Chomhairle Ealaíon, The Arts Council, Dublin.

Printed in Ireland by Colour Books Ltd.

Preface

On 7 April 1985 two books were launched at a reading
in Buswell's Hotel, Dublin 2. The books were "A Bright
Mask", new and selected poems by Robert Greacen, and
"Age of Exploration", a new collection of poems by Con-
leth Ellis. Both poets read from their work at the event.
These were the first two books to be published by the
newly-established Dedalus Press. By the end of 1991 the
press had published over fifty titles and established itself
as one of the leading poetry publishers in Ireland.

By now the emphases and direction of The Dedalus
Press are coming clear. There is a stress on poetry in
translation, and original poetry published tends towards
that same impetus in contemporary Ireland that faces a
wider world with its global problems and its artistic con-
cerns. Denis Devlin becomes a father figure in this area,
as does Brian Coffey.

Several of the younger Dedalus poets are also accom-
plished in the area of poetry translation and have publish-
ed translations of such poets as Agnes Nemcs Nagy
(Hungary), Mario Luzi (Italy), Tomas Tranströmer
(Sweden) and Marin Sorescu (Romania). The Dedalus
Press has also published an introductory volume to some
contemporary American poets, and a co-operative publi-
cation with Canada, a dual-language French Cana-
dian/Irish poets selection.

This anthology gathers together the best of the original
poetry published by The Dedalus Press since its inception.
It is intended as an overview of the work of the press, an

emphasis on the poets and poetry the press sees itself committed to, a proof that Irish poetry will not always confine itself to local dancehalls and farmyard intrigues. It hopes to offer a more vibrant view of Irish poets and their concerns than other anthologies have tended, in a sadly conservative mode, to suggest. It hopes to show that The Dedalus Press is up, and flying.

The collection tends to contain the quieter voices. It is an overtly limited anthology and does not make any claims to represent a country, a time or anything other than the work being offered by one small publishing house. The selections have been made, for the most part, by the poets themselves. As far as possible, each contributor has added some new work.

CONTENTS

ROBERT GREACEN

Robert Greacen was born in 1920, brought up in Belfast but spent most of his life in London. He has published many collections of his poetry, including the first book from The Dedalus Press, published in Dublin in April 1985, *A Bright Mask*, New and Selected Poems. He was acquainted with such poets as W.R.Rodgers and Patrick Kavanagh and he has been awarded bursaries by the Arts Council of Northern Ireland. In 1990 The Dedalus Press published, on the occasion of Robert's 70th birthday, a new collection *Carnival at the River*. In 1991 a short selection of his prose memoirs, *Brief Encounters*, was published by Cahair Books in Dublin.

Robert Greacen is now living in Dublin and has been made a member of Aosdána.

In the Belfast of the 1930's I was introduced at grammar school to lyric poetry via Palgrave's "Golden Treasury". Other school anthologies hinted at the existence of narrative and satire. I got the impression that, Masefield and Yeats and de la Mare apart, poets had to be dead. Poetry seemed to stop soon after the turn of the century.

Other boys had careers in mind: accountancy, law, medicine. My secret ambition was to be a journalist on the role model of the Belfast-born essayist Robert Lynd. As boys will, I rejected the notion of a safe job with a gold watch and a pension at 65.

Publication outside the school mag. came before I was 17 with an article on education in a fringe newspaper. It looked as if journalism would claim me. Then the War intervened, so ending my hopes of studying for a Diploma in Journalism at London University.

All was not lost. Someone showed me the "Listener" which printed 'free verse' poems. (Rhyme and metre had not greatly appealed to me.) I began to write poems in this mode and a few were accepted by "little mags".

However, it was not until I came across Auden, MacNeice, Spender, Eliot and Dylan Thomas at 18 or 19 that I was hooked by The White Goddess. Before I was 21 I had poems in "The Bell" and "Horizon", the most prestigious magazines in Dublin and London respectively. My first collection appeared under a London imprint in 1943. I was in the poetry business.

In my mid-thirties I ditched poetry. Or did poetry ditch me? The reasons are too complex to go into here. Unexpectedly at fifty plus I felt the urge again and created the character of Captain Fox. For nearly twenty years I've been writing poems again. Obviously the virus of my youth has not been eradicated.

I see poetry as an attempt to sort out the muddled events and impressions we call "life", a means of resolving or trying to resolve what Yeats termed "the quarrel with oneself". The important thing, I believe, is to want to write poems, not to want to be "a poet". Poets surely are dead.

- Robert Greacen

THE BIRD

A bird flew tangent-wise to the open window.
His face was a black face of black, unknowing death,
His eyes threw the grim glimt of sharpened stones
That children pile by unfrequented roads.

And that night, dreaming into a rapture of cardboard life,
I stared at the lean face of the bird:
A crow I think it was, but it was also death
And sure enough there was the crisp telegram next morning.

I placed my mirror to the flat, unfiltered light
But the razor cut me in spite of the guarantee,
And I knew it was not the razor but the ebony beak
That slashed the base of my left nostril.

I loved the man who lay in the cheap coffin.
It was he first showed me the damp, stereoscopic fields
Of County Down - and now he was away to farm
The curving acres of his jealous God.

I loved the ploughing of his sun-caught brow,
And the hay-lines and the chicken feathers in his hair
That was hay itself, the strongly cobbled boots
And the swaying, coloured idiom of his mind.

And now he was lying with the Holy Bible under his chin,
Sorry only to have died before harvest and turf-cutting,
Lying dead in the room of rafters and the grey, stopped clock-
 Because of the hatred of the bird I did not kill.

Sometimes now, years after, I am nakedly afraid in mid-winter
And ashamed to be afraid of an incessant beak
That raps a symphony of death on the window panes
Of the window I dare not throw wide open.

But one evening, just before I go to bed to die,
There will be the black face of black, unknowing death
Flying past my open window; there will be the black bird
With poison in his beak and hatred in his wings.

CAPTAIN FOX

Captain Fox sits reading metaphysics,
Hegel's the hundred watt bulb in his world.
Captain Fox is fond of Zürich's Hotel Excelsior.
"A reliable place", he says, "Solid, reliable."
He lights a Gauloise and blows a ring:
"One of these days I'll retire, I'm getting too old
For buggering along the autobahns.
Besides, I want to write a pre-Ayer work on philosophy
Which I'll publish at my own expense.
'Aspects of Hegel' or some such title.
Perhaps a village on the Adriatic..."

Basques, Catalans, Slovaks, Irishmen, Blacks,
These are Captain Fox's friends
Or perhaps, more exactly, business associates.
Luckily he's as much linguist as philosopher.
He talks for hours about fireworks
And the poetry of Rainer Maria Rilke.
Truly a civilized man, Captain Fox.

"Are you in business?" I once asked him.
"Well, let's say I provide...facilities."
A most civilised man, Captain Fox,
Discreet, solid, reliable.
His business isn't my business.

NOTES TOWARDS THE FOX BIOGRAPHY

Born in Cologne, 1920, father a Sergeant-Major
Serving in the British Army of Occupation;
Mother from Banbridge, Co Down, Pop. (1926) 5,000.
Youngest of the family, knew German before English,
Schooled throughout the British Isles without distinction
But nevertheless won an Exhibition to Oxford;
Never went near Cowley-cum-Dreaming-Spires
Because of some youthful love entanglement.

Joined the Army at Dad's suggestion,
But heard no angry shot in World War II,
Became an "Army intellectual" but could hold his own
At the outdoor pursuits of the upper classes.
Quickly assimilated officer class attitudes,
Soon promoted father to the rank of Major,
Seldom at a loss for answers to tricky questions.
Married a rich widow who died three years later.
Desk-bound, left the Army out of sheer boredom
But found the "Captain" handle useful in business.

Business? Ah, that's something I must research.
Occasional frantic journeys, exchange of sealed envelopes,
Entertains mostly in Hotel suites, no money worries.

I hope one day to fill these gaps.

MIDWINTER, W.11

Dragging afternoon in W.11 - cardboard sky, pink westerly;
Holland Park Avenue's treetops like dark lacework
Or witches' brooms upended in the flat grey light;
Dogcrap, litter, a film of damp on the pavements,
The down-at-heel streets of a decayed Empire,
The ebb and flow of phlegmatic traffic,
The slim London vowels of children loosed from school;
A blind man's stick pecks the zebra crossing.

Observe the Captain driving a Volvo up Campden Hill Road
Towards the terrace on the brow, near where the water tower
    stood
Before the speculators flailed it down in search of profit.
He carries a smart document case in Spanish leather
And rings the bell of a violet-doored, chic residence.
Carrington-Smythe of the F.O. lets him in, unspeaking.

Then two hours pass till Fox emerges, waves a goodbye;
Carrington-Smythe resumes his call to No. 10.
"GOVERNMENT MAY FALL" trumpets the *Evening Standard*.
But Fox has cooked the Opposition's goose
And steers his way westward into the stripling night.

FATHER AND SON

I can't remember how it happened,
How hatred seeded and grew rank,
A tall weed that dwarfed us both
And flourished till it stank.

Yet that isn't the whole story.
I remember evenings when, father and son,
We walked the velvety spring streets
And greeted the blossoms one by one.

Images come blurred, then clear
To harshness, violence; but still
Behind the bitter word, the angry gesture
I find the love that neither wished to kill.

Rest in peace, my father, trespass forgiven,
The dark stains whitened out. To-day
The siren screams our armistice,
The angry dwarfs ride fast away.

ONE DAY IN AUGUST

One day in August, going by bus to Annalong,
Past fields brown-pimpled with haycocks,
And whitewashed rectangular houses,
I tried - expatriate now - to overhear
The homely rhythms that my people use
As running murmur to a simple way of life.
Through their world's wilderness of tangled hate
I tried to see the obverse of the coins
That tinkle brash in every little till
And echo that intolerance I know too well.
Then came the answer on that August day:
If you would find the virtue of this place
Then search it out in tidy village streets
And in the narrow, stone-walled fields,
For there they build and work in quietness,
Far from the bigots' drumming rant
That stills the mind, that twists the heart.

JAMES JOYCE

Now we recall that bitter, dogged Dubliner, James Joyce,
Whose yeasty chaos travelled Europe in his aching brain.
Trieste, Zürich, Paris, Rome and other cities
Knew this young exile buoyed on anger and contempt
For all that was provincial, meanly self-sufficing.
A furnace blazed in his mind's core perpetually
And would not give him rest from constant labour
Until the multi-imaged soul cascaded many thousand words
Barbed and pristine with a febrile, love-hate energy.
Silence, exile, cunning - these sharp keys he cut
To unlock the obdurate gates to Europe,
These keys made in his Dublin prison in friend-wasted days
When Ibsen, Jonson, Hauptmann floodlit each chamber of his
    mind
And he determined not to honour those fierce claims
Of country, family and church: *I will not serve.*
Then think of him, half-blind and penniless in Eropean towns
Racked by the restive daemon of creativeness,
Showing a will inflexible against the little streets
With hatred in their piping, rabble voices,
He ceaselessly dredging an oceanic mind for images
To haunt our splintered century and show us to ourselves,
Crying aloud with all the anguish of our time.

BIRTHDAY

This day my birthday and the autumn trees
Stand to attention in their gilded uniforms.
These tall guardsmen, inspected closely,
Show tarnished epaulettes, loose buttons,
Trunks battle-scarred in windy skirmishes,
Boughs and branches sooty, furred with dust,
Green battledress soiled from enemy assault.

The air is calm today, bland and unstirred,
Everywhere the sour odour of torn leaves rises
To greet the ghosts that shamble in for carnival,
The All Souls gala of the restless dead.

There was a foreigner who loved these streets
Who walked among our summer-suited trees
Observing man and leaf with zealous eye,
Trying to will himself into our alien tongue.
He died in Bietigheim a month ago
And now lies quiet in his Swabian clay.
Helmut, good friend, answer my questions:
Can a seed die? Does a tree perish?
Is there light at the root of darkness?
I am listening, Helmut, listening for answers
In the deep stillness of my heart's autumn,
Hearing only stray murmurs of vast silences
On this my birthday. Yet listening, listening.

TIN FLOWERS

The old Mexican woman
Hobbles in the street:
"Tin flowers for graves,
Pretty, best quality.
Flores para los muertos,
Coronas para los muertos".

Their brilliance shatters my eyes.
Hepatitis, cancer, malaria, syphilis,
Come take your pick, good sirs,
Red, blue, yellow, green.

"Beautiful flowers, pure tin flowers,
I shall not rob you,
Colours of the rainbow,
Buy Maria's flowers".

I empty my trouser pockets
Throw my loose change at her,
And she grins and grins,
Bows to the generous señor,
Opens the cavern of her mouth
To pour out a hoarse aria:
"Flores para los muertos,
Coronas para los muertos".

CARNIVAL AT THE RIVER

The procession of ghosts shuffles by.
Faceless, bannerless, blobs in a landscape
Of dead trees, rotted flowers.
Gradually the blobs dissolve into people.
Father steps out in Edwardian style
Links arms with mother in her flowered hat.
There's cousin Jim, his gun lusting for snipe.

Aunt Tillie's fox fur dangles at her neck.
Teachers pace by in funereal gowns,
Boys in uniform, bare-kneed, sulk past
As if they'd been cheated of a holiday.
Stewart pushes a 1930's Raleigh bike,
Willie McIlwaine drools over an oval ball.
I turn on my side and hope for easy sleep
Away from the images of childhood
But the procession sidles into dream.
I am walking beside grandfather.
He plucks his beard, tells me softly:
"We're going to the carnival.
We are gathering at the river."
I feel cold, my guts tighten.
Father's father, take my arm!
Grandfather holds me, quotes Beckett:
"Je n'ai rien contre les cimetières".
We laugh, walk arm in arm to the carnival.
The gathering at the river.

ST. ANDREW'S DAY, 1985

St. Andrew's Day, blind November fumbling
The hurt leaves, bleached gutter orphans.
Half-light domesticates raw brick.
A mediocre day, not to be remembered.
It's 2 p.m. at Ladbroke Grove. I board a bus.
The mourners are gathering at Glengarriff.
Is it drizzling there? I hear the rain
Touchtyping an elegy on the Bay waters.
Though in her will she said "No flowers"
Our daughter will place veronica on the coffin
Borne through the woods to the old Killeen.

Will the funeral go to plan, discreetly,
Even in the drizzle I imagine falling
On the lands of Gael and Planter?
I say a London goodbye to a lost wife,
Remember our time of roses, promises,
The silvered sea at Ardnagashel,
Earrings of fuchsia in the hedgerows,
Hope arching like a rainbow over all.

DRUMMOND ALLISON 1921-1943

(Killed in action on the Garigliano, Italy, 2/12/43)

Your voice is with me now.
Its confident Home Counties' tone
Sounds across a fifty-year divide.
Your khaki figure walks a Belfast street
Intent on jaunt and enterprise.
We weave among the statues round the City Hall
Then ride east across the Albert Bridge.
Laughs fall like coins into the Lagan.
You talk of Keyes and John Heath-Stubbs
Young Oxford friends - Keyes marked for death -
Of girls you lusted for in vain.
We spend an evening at the Opera House
Then sink young men's despair in pints
Of collared Guinness at "The Crown".
You write from hospital - "trench mouth" -
You disappear and letters cease.
Your mother sends "The Yellow Night"
A poet's will and testament.
I read the slip framed in dark blue:
"From Drummond Allison with love."
I shiver at your mother's words:
"I very much regret ... "

CONLETH ELLIS

Conleth Ellis was born in Carlow in 1937. He published many collections of his poetry, both in English and in Irish. He taught in Athlone, Co Westmeath. He was chairman of Poetry Ireland at the time of his death in 1988 and helped build up the society in its early years. The sophistication of his poetry was praised by Austin Clarke; Augustine Martin placed him in the front rank of a bilingual generation that has created a flowering of poetic talent. His polished, controlled and passionately engaged poetry has been sadly neglected. His collection "Age of Exploration" was the second book published by The Dedalus Press and in 1989 The Dedalus Press published his collection"Darkness Blossoming". The poem "Sepia Print" won first prize in the poetry section of the Irish-Australian literary competition sponsored by the Northern Bank (Ireland) Ltd., and was published in the Irish Times.

GRAVES

A grey squirrel in the morning sits
On the lawn I have long since mowed
This summer's final time. He sets
Ambivalently about digging, earth clawed

To a shallow tomb where he buries
Nothing, being too enamoured of frost
That smoulders in sun the upper storeys
Of chestnuts strain from the east.

I brace myself against a sudden brand
That sets alight a memory, and watch
Long lost children on a lawn pretend
At pirates. We would mine a ditch,

Entomb tin boxes filled with dice,
A pencil, bottle tops, a copper coin,
And even when we knew to mark the place
We never found them when we dug again.

Are we the things we have forgotten? Do
Our lowland pasts crumble particle
By molecule and year by day
To clay stratified against the vertical

Tyranny of now? Sleep, squirrel, winter
Into spring, memory honed against decease.
Both of us can hear the chestnuts' banter
With a sun come only now to reminisce.

AGE OF EXPLORATION

Now suddenly on your map
I have no coordinates.
Somewhere to the left
Under the western angel's
Blast from puffed cheeks
Where the cartographer wrote
HERE BE MONSTERS
I have been banished.

Another dark age begins
And there is no anticipating
The ritual preparations
For a voyage of discovery.
There must be endless ruined delay
Before our hearts' conquistadores
Find for themselves a country
Beyond the intimacies of love.

Nor will this mark an end
Of our probing of bounds.
Is there the coast of a sixth
Continent to be charted and
Are there fathoms still to be set
Against an eighth sea's shoals?
Best if love map out its course
Only as far as the edges of hope.

ROCK POOL

This child on hunkers at the edge of rocks
Looks right through her own reflection,
Through clouds pressed flat on the sky,
Watches the wine anemone's mouth softly
Open. Her poetry is the colour of stones,
Creatures whose pulse is the beat of tides,
Hidden places beyond the pool's bright skin.

If I were in her poem I would not see
Her enamelled eyes, her lip fast in her teeth,
The reversed parting of her dampened hair.
And she might glimpse my figure leaning
Over her shoulder and not look through it
As now at some crab burrowing in sand,
Trailing an age's growth of sea-green weed.

TRYST

Push the door open with your finger tips
(I have oiled the hinges beyond a whisper)
And you will discover me, book in hand,
Sitting by the window, pretending to read,
Feigning surprise at your visiting.

Excuse the lightness of banter to muffle
(I will move about to disguise a tremor)
The thud of a heart's machined insistence,
And the hand marking my place in the book
Will point you towards a favourite chair.

I will see you try to hide how you see
Through all my elaborately nonchalant ease,
And you will say you happened to be passing,
And the ritual lines of our dance
Bit by bit will shorten. O please come.

IN THE BEGINNING

Agama lizard on a rock, second
by second changing the world.

The purple head nodding approval
in rhythm with a new creation.

The rock, hurled huge as a hill
from a volcano's dispassionate

heart, red-hot ages past, warm
to the dragon skin of the feet.

Only the wedge of the head,
it seems, surviving petrifaction,

and in the head the guileless eyes,
and in the eyes the murderous tongue.

All the Serengeti deafened with heat,
each crushed noise a tiny stain.

Artefact of eternity, mechanical,
or sculpted from a precious resin

secreted in the ducts of time,
Agama lizard suddenly vanished,

fluid as a silverfish tumbled
from a book haphazardly opened.

The world ending second by second.
The rock denying it was ever there.

MIRAGE

All morning we have driven through the Serengeti
and now landscape to left and to right of us
is turning to water in the middle distance
to trees and their reflections in a lake
shimmering in tiny waves in the corner of the eye.

Towards noon we pass a man who is sitting
alone under a lone baobab tree's shade
and know how we have seemed to him in our coming
for miles out of the haze and for minutes of time
and how he may ponder our going again
into a world beyond the pale of the tree's reality.

He shows us the palm of a hand by way of salute.

FLIGHT HOME

(I laugh with my teeth but my heart is bleeding - proverb)

Spears are not allowed in the cabin, the hostess
said. These will have to go in the cargo hold.

At the airport a drum cavorts on the carousel,
absurd legs in the air, like a stuck pig.
It will be a coffee table, a conversation piece
in a drawingroom deep in the suburban bush.

Do you think they will know how to tune it,
heating it exactly to the tensions needed
for a dance to set hips dizzily spinning,
feet stamping, arms whirling frenzies of delight?

This *nanga's* strings, will they ever be plucked?
Who is likely to breathe joy or grief
or the secret talk of love into this curved flute?
A child may take, naughtily, the rattle gourd

from its nail on a wall and break the silence,
but the silence soon must return, gaping down
from the great dead eyes of the priests' masks
neatly hung, dramatically lit in a hallway.

An elephant foot umbrella stand is carted away
to a taxi by a woman in a safari suit and a hat
with a leopard skin band and several bracelets
of elephant hair as amulets against the traffic.

Everything is here, except for the people,
the people who sang for harvest and rain,
for luck in the hunt, at birth and at death,
at marrying and burying, when the music called.

You know the smith recited a poem invoking success
making these spears at the forge in the magic fire?

CREED

Though a moon that shone
Ivory in a north sky
Roughly washed with lye
Has all but gone,

A cloud's edge says, Faith
Is the only prayer
To countenance despair;
Know by the fading wraith

In the branches' snare
That the sun turns
Still and the dark burns
Into the light somewhere.

FROM A SEPIA PRINT

For Corporal John P.O'Donnell, 10th Battn., 1st Div., Australian Forces, poet, and Thomas H.O'Donnell, 20th Battn., Australian Infantry, killed near Westhoek, 28 Sept., 1917, aged 26 years, twin brothers, of South Australia and Carlow, Ireland.

It is the small birds of Hampshire now
Singing the old, glad songs in all the trees
Round Netley Hospital. You convalesce, Jack,
After France and Egypt and Gallipoli,
Locked in a silent dream
Of the whining sky and the death scream.

It is the small birds of Hampshire now
Weaving from memory a seamless cloak
For you to wear, Jack, against the cold
Of a brother killed in Flanders,
The twin your life has worn
Always like a wild flower, blighted and torn.

You write an elegy full of the tropical night,
Of space and stars and longings
Without end or beginning, McCarthy's Creek
In your mind and the gaunt gumtrees,
The kookaburra's cry,
Almond in bloom against an adopted sky.

You write an elegy loud with the breath of life,
Flanagan's rowdy bar by the Wallaby Track,
The teamsters sparring and Old Mulga Bill
Cracking a rawhide thong, a sail
Snapped full above the waves,
Music jostling in Naracoorte's wild caves.

Jack, your Anzac songs are scored to turn
Some part of the madness to a sanity
Of rhyme and humour and contained lament.
Wild geese climbed October winds to cross
Cold hills of Sari Bahir.
Imbros was pinned to the sea like a jewelled star.

Mounds moulded to the swollen dead,
Bleached bones of Troy, lost villages,
Lost girls, straggles of roses opening to heal
A ruined mill. Do you remember too
The first birdsong of home
Falling like rain into your waking room

In a childhood Carlow till you rose
And climbed with Tom on the window ledge
To look into the apple-coloured light
Behind the Greenbank gates, to plan
Adventures, endless play
To shake delights from the secret folds of day?

The boys your games made into heroes then
Marched Carlow's streets in ranks behind
A different drum while you were leaving
Your new stars behind in a southern night
To squat under the shells
That bruised your hopes in the vice-tight Dardanelles.

Twice exiled, when the guns are stopped
A month from now and winter holds
The hedgerows close in an urgent search
For shreds of love to hang against a spring,
You will not come back
To walk the measured silence of the Barrow Track.

It is the small birds of Hampshire now
Repeating and repeating that you won't
Face again into the setting sun
Or set your feet towards the streets of youth.
You will turn south once more
And haul half of the wrecked dream safely ashore.

FIRST POINT OF ARIES

It will be too late when flowers
Scorch holes in the wind
To say, This is to be young,
Is spring. It is spring when
Scents on air like spikenard, lights
Like quartz, say the imago is come
After all metamorphoses to live a day
That will change the tincture of breath
And drop in the earth a spore
To breed shoots of the hellebore
Against a longlived death.

JOHN F. DEANE

John F. Deane was born in Achill Island, County Mayo, in 1943.
In 1979 he founded Poetry Ireland, the National Poetry Society.
He is a full-time writer and has edited "The Cold Heaven"
(Wolfhound Press 1990), an anthology of questioning religious
poetry by Irish poets. His poetry collections are "Stalking After
Time" (1977), "High Sacrifice" (1981), "Winter in Meath", (1985),
"Road, with Cypress and Star" (1988) and "The Stylized City",
new and selected poems, (1991).

I came late to poetry, being an islandman, and though I rushed at it with the excitement that came from reading Hopkins's "Wreck of the Deutschland", still I have been slow, regretting the initial flush, reaching laboriously for an understanding of what poetry is to me. The island God with whom I was brought up has left deep, perhaps ineradicable, urges within me; having lost contact with Him - the way one sheds youth, with regret - I look through poetry for another, hopefully truer, version of God.

Like many of my generation I spent some years trying out the religious vocation; I do not regret those years but I have always found them difficult to locate in whatever imaginative interpretation of life poetry is to offer. After Hopkins I drifted quickly, through an unsatisfactory flirtation with Kavanagh, towards the beautifully harsh realities of R.S.Thomas. I see him as having explored with exceptional honesty and through deftly sculpted poems that difficult area of doubt in which I move. Back home there was always Thomas Kinsella, whose poetry I return to the way I return, whenever I can, to the Atlantic, for sustenance, to touch again what is most native, most personal, most honest and demanding in the psyche.

Suddenly one day I discovered Tomas Tranströmer, the Swedish poet; in his work I found a searching and a form that answered my own aspirations and most importantly of all I think I discovered a liberating force for my own imagination, a permeability, a way to shove the desperate search for meaning aside and allow words themselves their natural force, let the imagination speak without the impulses of intellection interfering. An extreme version of this kind of poetry I have discovered in Jorie Graham, the American poet. Perhaps one finds one's own voice only after a long engagement with many others.

- John F. Deane

PENANCE

They leave their shoes, like signatures, below;
above, their God is waiting. Slowly they rise
along the mountainside where rains and winds go
hissing, slithering across. They are hauling up

the bits and pieces of their lives, infractions
of the petty laws, the little trespasses and
sad transgressions. But this bulked mountain
is not disturbed by their passing, by this mere

trafficking of shale, shifting of its smaller stones.
When they come down, feet blistered, and sins
fretted away, their guilt remains and that black
mountain stands against darkness above them.

ON A DARK NIGHT

On a dark night
When all the street was hushed, you crept
Out of our bed and down the carpeted stair.
I stirred, unknowing that some light
Within you had gone out, and still I slept.
As if, out of the dark air

Of night, some call
Drew you, you moved in the silent street
Where cars were white in frost. Beyond the gate
You were your shadow on a garage-wall.
Mud on our laneway touched your naked feet.
The dying elms of our estate

Became your bower
And on your neck the chilling airs
Moved freely. I was not there when you kept
Such a hopeless tryst. At this most silent hour
You walked distracted with your heavy cares
On a dark night while I slept.

WINTER IN MEATH

to Tomas Tranströmer

Again we have been surprised,
deprived, as if suddenly,
of the earth's familiarity;

it is like the snatching away of love
making you aware at last you loved;

sorrows force their way in, and pain,
like memories half contained;

the small birds, testing boldness,
leave delicate tracks closer
to the back door

while the cherry flaunts blossoms of frost
and stands in desperate isolation.

*

The base of the hedgerow is a cliff of snow,
the field is a still of a choppy sea,
white waves capped in a green spray;

a grave was dug into that hard soil
and overnight the mound of earth
grew stiff and white as stones flung onto a beach;

our midday ceremony was hurried,
forced hyacinths and holly wreathes dream birds
appearing on our horizonless ocean;

the body sank slowly, the sea
closed over, things on the seabed
stirred again in expectation.

*

This is a terrible desolation -

the word "forever"
stilling all the air

to glass.

*

Night tosses and seethes;
mind and body chafed all day
as a mussel-boat restlessly
irritates the mooring;

on estuary water a fisherman
drags a long rake against the tide;
one snap of a rope and boat and this
solitary man
sweep off together into night;

perhaps the light from my window
will register a moment with some god
riding by on infrangible glory.

*

At dawn
names of the dead
appear on the pane

beautiful
in undecipherable frost;

breath
hurts them
and they fade.

*

The sea has gone grey as the sky
and as violent;

pier and jetty go under
again and again
as a people suffering losses;

a flock of teal from the world's edge
moves low over the water
finding grip for their wings along the wind;

already, among stones, a man, like a priest,
stooping in black clothes, has begun beachcombing;

the dead, gone silent in their graves,
have learned the truth about resurrection.

*

You can almost look into the sun
silver in its silver-blue monstrance
cold over the barren white cloth of the world;

for nothing happens;

each day is an endless waiting
for the freezing endlessness of the dark;

once - as if you had come across
a photograph, or a scarf maybe -
a silver monoplane like a knife-blade cut
across the still and haughty sky

but the sky healed up again after the passing
that left only a faint, pink thread,
like a scar.

REVOLUTIONS OF THE HEAVENLY BODIES

The circus, in Leningrad, is a cupola,
a cathedral dome; as a child I thought
a man made rocket might burst through the stretched
hide of the sky and the words come back "yes yes!
oh yes!" Dogs dressed as maids waltz for us,
chimps push each other round in prams,

an elephant goes down upon its knees to pray;
the air is brass, the quickening tympanum
lifts our eyes heavenward; beauty lilts along
an invisible line above us; almost naked
- the welcoming buttocks, the challenging
passages between - she walks among constellations.

Father chats in Russian with a guard; he has gone
beyond the frontier, abandoning me again.

LOVE-POEM; LEITRIM

A spattering of sloes against the sky;
stars sharp as thorns and as sudden;
over the valley's crotch a witch's shark-tooth moon;
I hear the cracking of littlest bones

between the jaws of night predators
whose unseen, watching eyes are insolent, and round.
A blue flush on the sloe's skin
comes away with the touch of a finger;

sometimes, after love, I lay my head
quietly on the hills of her breasts,
dreading cold that will enter limbs

with a sound as of glass shattering,
and the angel's lifted finger
singling me out, berry, frost-petal, skull.

THE STYLIZED CITY

I, John, I was on the island ...

Fishing-nets were woven round the coffins
and Latin words rolled over them, like breakers
falling in among the people, drenching them;

tall pallid candles stood in rows;
the women's lips moved soundlessly, the men
squeezed up their caps in their red fists.

The sun was streaming through the crafted windows,
touching the walls with fluctuant colours :
jasper, amethyst, carnelian;

and high in the rose window the Heavenly City,
stylized, its walls on twelve foundation stones
and souls rising towards it on ships of gold.

How the heart lifts towards such light! though I know
it is artifice, the fervour the poet dreamed
was a voice like the sound of the ocean, that called:

write down all that you see into a book.

MACHENRY'S GENERAL STORE

The fire, collapsing into mounds, coal shapes
shifting, for comfort, listing;
a moist log is a forest after rain
with a thrush whistling;

we lie down, under the weight of night, to rest,
form hillocks, humps, plains;
we settle gently into blackness,
or the grey light of dreams.

When the general store started up in flames
it was past midnight, and very cold;
we gathered, gratefully, to share
an unexpected festival;

the family stood in nightclothes, in a huddle,
wrapped in neighbours' coats,
held firmly round the shoulders;
everyone, they said, is out;

paint-tins exploded, canisters of gas,
windows, the roof, the doors,
geysers of flame, volcanoes, sudden fountains of sparks.
On the second floor

Tom had made coffins with a craftsman's care,
each one, he said, a work of art;
we imagined them, flatbottomed rowboats of fire,
crackling apart;

the planed, bone-white beams,
the suavely polished, outfitted body,
crucifixes in their boxes, gleaming,
the waiting name-plates, with the R.I.P.

Tom scared us, his mumbling words,
his gruffness, his scars, his stumps and limp;
a misfired shotgun blasted his fingers,
a nostril, his upper lip;

coffin-lids leaned languidly against a wall,
he would gather one, like a dancing partner,
deliver a coffin reluctantly, missing its small
individual character ...

"Tom!" - screams, and "Tom's in there! Tom! Tom! Tom!"
Silence; the fire's labouring.
For days they sifted the ash, its hillocks, its dream,
 - nothing;

rain came at last;
the ashes hissed, became mud;
nothing - not Tom, nor coffin, nor the brass
figure of the crucified.

THE GAME

You came into the game
from a starting-point near rocks
and ran, trying to reach the stone
placed at the centre, the den, the safehouse, home;

and there I go -
screaming round the outermost circle,
father pounding after,
a switch of sea-wrack in his hand.

Eternity, he told me, is like the letter O,
it has no beginning and no end;
or like the naught, perhaps,
and you could slither down and down

through its black centre.
With a silver pin
he drew the periwinkles from their shells,
soft flesh uncoiling from the whorl;

he scooped out gravelly meat from the barnacle,
swallowed its roundness whole, with that black
mucous-like blob at its centre;
and there I go, half-nauseated,

following;
the way you become your father,
that same diffidence and turning inwards,
that same curving of the spine,

the way the left shoulder lifts in emphasis;
and here I am,
pounding round the outermost circle,
a switch of sea-wrack in my hands.

NOVICE

Postulant, the way you start into a book,
with zeal, into the holocaust of self; O God
who out of living and elect stones ...

I will soak in wisdom, to be made whole.

I was beckoned in to the harness shed;
the brother stood, red-faced, jocular and poised,
a sheep held fast between his knees,

the grey-white wool matted and soiled,
the eyes far-seeing. I held her, gently,
and she skittered and dragged from me,

hooves slithering across the cobblestones;
a humane killer, drill-perfect, primed,
was touched to the skull, the trigger touched;

I imagined the bullet eating
like a bit through bone; the suddenness
took me, the instantly yielded weight,

and we fell, together, at the brother's feet;
I was sent back to the flower-beds and grass verges;
come! chapter one, book one, in the beginning God ...

PATRICK DEELEY

Born in Co. Galway in 1953, he is a teacher in a primary school
in Ballyfermot, Dublin. His poems have appeared widely; his
first collection, "Intimate Strangers", appeared in 1986 and in
1990 The Dedalus Press published his collection, "Names for
Love".

The pheasant's usually most vocal at dusk, making a sound like a hiccup, as if he were drunk with sunset.

And that's the only sound he makes, but it is memorable.

I heard it first and often in the marshland near my parents' house in East Galway, the place where I tried to lose and find, forget and remember myself as a child.

Years later I attempted these paradoxes through poems. And as I changed, so too did the poetry.

Now Dublin is my home; it presents its own set of frictions between person and place!

The marsh, a quaking mire in every weather, is all but drained.

And the poems? Maybe they're draining too!

What matter! Long as they occur to me and regardless of the guise of place, I'll be trying, like the pheasant, to say myself memorably.

Patrick Deeley

CLEANING TREES

The spade felt heavy and fat in my child-grip.
Still I swung it one-handed, pretending
to be a hunter as I moved through the wood.

My job was to clean each tree
marked with an X, so that the saw could cut
below ground-level, capture the curve
of spreading roots. Looking now
at the sturdy upthrust of a stately ash,
I knew its worth in hurleys.

The bole served as fulcrum for my
levering spade. I scraped off ivy and moss,
scooped out clay and grit, accidentally nicking
the stained bark. Careless strokes
on ivorine roots rebounded as shocks.

I paused to survey my spadework:
tenacious anchors partly exposed,
gouged out earth resembling a grave,
this specimen doomed by its perfect physique
while flawed trees about it would live.

I located another tree, my pace quickened
by the rising moan of the chainsaw
gaining ground. Suddenly a lizard slapped
across the stabbing spade. I picked it up,
sadly studied its green length
tapering to a miniature dragon-tail.

Stories of fire-breathing monsters I had read,
vivid enough for child-belief,
must have evolved, I presumed,
from creatures harmless as this -
just as gnomes, witches, a whole assembly
of oddities from folktale and legend,
probably had as their origin
nothing more extraordinary than stunted trees
in dark woods. I weighed the lizard

limp-lifeless in my hand, settled it -
on a tussock. To my amazement then,
it flicked and was grass. I went back
to the cleaning of trees with new heart.

LOWRY

It's as though an old jerky Chaplin movie
of men with bowler hats, umbrellas, and boots,
had been stilled by Lowry's unsentimental wit
and oiled on canvas in ridiculous ballet.
Only the architectures are majestic: the mills,
domes, smoking stacks, overseeing everything;
the bright windows of churches and mosques
hinting at mysteries; the Stockport Viaduct
elevated to represent grandeur and strength.
Dogs ramble through scenes; a cat looks on.
Here are the cripples, and here the bearded lady -
human misfortunes and the human predicament
objectised. There is work and recreation,
his characters caught in 'twenties-style dress,
ant-men, antics, amid the grime and gloom
of an industrial landscape. Sometimes the figures
assemble on platforms, in waiting rooms,
about the scene of an accident or a fight,
but this is their only contact, each islanded
and intrinsically alone, as is the artist,
self-portrayed with red eyes and frenzied face,
or suggesting his crucifixion in a lamp post.

BASEMENT

Glad of my escape, I still wonder
how the new occupant is faring.
Each evening I pause while passing
the old redbrick house, and scan

its basement. Usually a light glows
behind the window bars, and a man's
bowed figure is visible, his shoulders
hunched, elbows leaning on a table.

Sometimes his fingers tap-dance
in a toil of idleness or boredom,
or he moves to retrieve something,
moves as though lumbered by oppression.

Is it the notion of so many rooms,
their lives and luggage, a whole house
propped on him, has tensed his mind,
cast him in the role of Atlas?

I wonder if telltale sounds from
overhead still pierce the ceiling
or if ho omploys tactics like mine,
letting his imagination flesh out

each voice, step, bedsqueak, doorslam,
in a sense redeeming angle-cramped
living. And when he encounters
fellow-occupants, on domestic errands,

do they stop and talk, or does that
reticence I was party to still stand,
permitting them only to smile with
the shyness of intimate strangers?

ENCOUNTER

The slug and the spent condom
glistening here side by side
on a dew-dampened park bench
could hardly be mistaken
for one another, slack artifice
at odds with plump nature,
yet both are cleansing agents.

An old man standing near,
noticing what I've noticed
berates: *Is there no shame
left in the world? To think
such godless dirty conduct
goes on in public now -
I tell you it's a disgrace!*

Something's always comical
about the flustered face
of righteous indignation,
and something's reprehensible
even in safe acts of casual sex
on park benches, but I keep
my silence and a steady gaze,

for sake of all the years,
their differing impulses.
Momentarily now, the slug
nuzzles, then starts to retreat
from both offending sheath
and sudden lamp of sunlight,
being, in its way, sensible.

THE PICTURES

The white protagonist pressed
square-jawed and zealous
past mudhuts where natives oozed
admiration and bewilderment;

pressed fearless into jungle,
speckled distances ashiver
with mire and python, feverish
drone of sun-fed creatures

lapsing into sudden silence
which a host of arrows dispersed -
loosed by savages stood
ebon and still behind trees!

Luck contrived to save him,
his ambushers proving in need
of more stringent practice,
though close shaves thudded

impressively into wood. He,
armed only in righteousness,
swung into swashbuckling action,
coolly dislodging his enemies.

And we, bunched in paint-flecked
musty seats, hoodwinked
by his depiction as hero,
went on supporting the villain.

LEFT-HANDED

In the original sense *lyft,*
meaning *weak* or *worthless,*
the Concise Oxford says.
Now listed as *clumsy, awkward,*
double-edged, ambiguous.

Normally the less used hand.
I'd say *usually,* Lexicon!
Innocents were persecuted
because of it once, even burned
as witches at the stake.

Morganatic. I trace this back
to Germanic custom where
the man of high rank
who married the woman of low
gave her his left hand

and, on the morning after
consummation, a gift which alone
of all his possessions
or titles could be
inherited by her children.

I find other words
uncomplimentary to left-handedness:
the glib dismissive *gauche*
of the French, the unfortunate
sinister of Latin origin,

and the one I know best,
ciotóg, directed at me
out of the side of the mouth
by teacher or fellow-pupil
in early oak-desk days.

That slur on small difference -
I'm almost grateful to it now
for catching me up
in the first fierce clench
to familiarity with life.

Torn-out transcriptions,
crumpled veins of blue and red,
my nonconformist hands
beaten on the anvil-rule,
yet refusing to be forged.

Fights afterwards in the yard
with boys who tried to impose
their own coercive law -
none could easily best me;
I was clumsy, awkward, southpaw.

GHOST

The neighbourhood's appalled
at the allocation
of a house to the ghost.

Some people close their eyes,
pretend he doesn't exist.
Others dredge up

the old accusations about
chains jangling, scrap
being thrown around the place.

They say he doesn't keep
himself well; in truth,
the stain of their prejudice

shows through his whiteness.
they resent his irregular
lifestyle, the way he vanishes

into his former existence
for weeks on end,
only to materialise again,

making a mockery - they say -
of walls, and, by extension,
of all solid meanings.

He says why shouldn't walls
be there to serve him,
rather than he them,

puts his disappearances
down to business
and the pull that's always

possessed him
since first the tribe
was interfered with by spells.

Gone on his summer-rambles
when hotheads burn
his house to the ground,

appalling the neighbourhood
in the glare that follows
into saying the right things.

Now he's ditched again
under bare wintry bushes -
you can hear in passing

his huddled children
haunting the darkness
with their cries and sneezing.

CATAPULT

He dreams of slaying Goliath.
Who Goliath is he doesn't know,
except that he's a giant
so huge as to be everywhere

at once, and therefore difficult
to see properly or to hit
where it counts. Meanwhile,
he practices on other targets:

pigeons, for example, although
he likes pigeons, or pities them
to be more exact. Their red feet
prancing on the pavement,

the changing sheen of colours
braceleting their necks,
strike chords in his heart
which make him act rough.

So he sets a pebble in the patch
pen-knifed from an old tyre,
draws the elastic taut,
aims at wing or breast, and

twang! His finger vibrates,
the victim flaps grudgingly off.
Dustbins, lamp-posts, railings,
whet his aim and appetite.

One whole day he shoots
onto the sheer ice of a lake
that grew in the park with winter,
for the way a stone can skate

far out towards the centre.
Nightfall pulls him back
through the estates. *Kylemore,
Bluebell,* naming the rural past,

tag incongruously along.
He eyes the green-glass globules
that high overhead take in
the pulsing cables on pylons

close by the cluttered canal.
Inspiration hits, like lightning.
Limbs strain, mind grows calm,
as he climbs the sparred

skeletal symmetry of steel,
all noise and distraction pared
to a thin singing that is tangible
as the wind, but more consistent.

He stands transfigured
by the flare of electric wires,
in that moment certain he has seen
Goliath frowning, as if stung.

THE BOOK

Well might you say of us -
my baby daughter, myself,
cheeked smooth with unshaven -
that we are blood-close,
eyeing from opposite ends
the picture book of youth.

Bone-match, blond complexions,
both our heads thatched
a scant yet exact pattern
now and for the last time -
she thrives, I am dwindling,
this no mere happenstance

but laid out, immutable.
In her the world's newly made
(fish, animals, trees, birds),
so naturally I let it pass
between us without weeping.
She points, mouths the words.

GERARD SMYTH

Gerard Smyth was born in Dublin in 1951 where he works as a journalist with *The Irish Times*. He has published three full-length collections of poetry, including "Painting the Pink Roses Black" from The Dedalus Press in 1986. Recent poetry has been published in journals and magazines in Ireland and abroad.

HEN WOMAN

You cross yourself when you're told
that forklightning scorched a man
in the next parish, left a wall scarred
and made a silhouette of straw and stone.

After the downpour
soft ground is cooking in the sun,
rainwater floats on cold enamel.
After a night of augury
your apron pockets fatten with eggs
collected from haystack and dunghill.

Balancing unspilled water in two buckets
full to the brim
is a trick learned in youth:
you perform it well,
your knuckles turning to the colour of iodine.

In shadows of furniture you are left
remembering that the meek
shall inherit the earth. It's a simple world
of right and wrong. Gold wears off the rim of the cup
you drink from.

GHOST FORGE

A nest of nails where hammers descended
striking iron,
releasing an iron fragrance.
Where stains of fire proliferated
the anvil's withered down to its roots.

The pitcher under the water-tap
has a chipped mouth.
Ash scooped out of the brazier
shall never cool
nor shall the glow on the forehead
of the horseshoe-maker.

Sparks that fluttered, dazzling his eyes,
have become still now,
stored up as embers in the folds of an apron.
The bellows' breath is gone,
dried up in the pungence of smoke.

REMINISCENCE

1 Evensong

From the door I saw unending distance,
crossroads where nothing happened.
It seemed like the age before cars.

The comforting noise of milk filling a bucket
came from the shadow-world.
It was milking-time in the country,
the hour I loved. Darkness crowded the henhouse,
I was afraid to enter. The bolt was drawn
to guard against the prowling vixen.

2 Childhood House

In the kitchen everything shone:
linoleum, china, the stacked dresser.
Smoke discoloured the wall it clung to
and the hearthstone under the dreaming dog.

Grandmother - her ages of grief thickening -
had a deep distrust of electricity.
With great patience she combed the hair
falling to her shoulders.

Late at night
dance-music rose up from the wooden radio.
The calmed-down fire forsaken until cock-crow
was enough to keep the chill outside
in the crevices
and treetops brimming with heaven's breeze.

LONELINESS

Rain sings a requiem in the knacker's yard.
At the edge of wasteland
a child's plaything is discarded, suddenly
and forever. Instead of smoke
chimneys shed the soul-stifling melancholy
of nights at the end of June.

The clock strikes; its twelve chimes hypnotise.
Over an unfinished game of chess
someone says Goodnight. The light
of the apple-blossom is snatched away.
Watchdogs blend with the quiet behind closed windows.

Everyone's at rest
except the girl sewing moonbeams to a garment.
The house of glass glowing in the dark
is the last bus with only a few travellers
going back to where they began.

LOVERS

We lie down and the walls rise up.
The lurking mouse discovers nothing edible
in the cupboards. On your bare back
the moon has dropped the pallor of its face.

Nails and hammer, shovel and pick
have been put aside. The hush is diaphanous
and broken only by the bark
of a dog which can't keep its voice in its mouth.

We are never prepared for that sudden visit
of sound to our ears. Behind closed eyelids
there's nothing to be heard. How empty the world is
and in it the gigantic throbbing of our hearts,

the stillness is the gesture of things in common -
like the stillness in the belly of the Trojan Horse.

FEVER

The windows of the hospital reflect a lunar calm.
Nightsmoke from the boiler-house
swirls in muted agitation. In a corner
of the fever-ward geraniums that were wilting
bloom - it is the only miracle,
the only sign of a life not thwarted by lassitude.

Soup thick as ointment broods in a bowl,
stiffened bread lies mouldering. The silence now
is a nightingale empty of sound.
The sick child wakes after falling
through the deepness of space:
he feels the leadweight of eyelids
half-opening to the present. At midnight,
when the youngest face wears the oldest expression,
the dark is perfect:
  - it paints the pink roses black.

TEMPLE

1

Whose eyes are these that gaze and gaze
from sculpted solitude
- fading from icon and pieta?

It is getting dark.
Dusk has half-erased the house of God.
From nowhere comes the voice
of supplication, pleading
at the edge of light and refuge.

Out of the depths and from echoing hill
earth's cries
invoke the unsealed sepulchre
   where death consoles the living.

2

Silencing all questions
the smoke of incense hoists a chant
of joyous Easter Latin.

Brass and bronze have the appearance of gold.
The bones of statues
are radiant in light from another world.

The entry door looms up -
when it opens the air divides,
wisps of air breathe down the nave
of brooding quietness.

Stone rises to reach the sky.
Where sunlight collides with chapel glass
a hermit stands in fire
reciting, perhaps, the last of the psalms.

INTERLUDE

Looking at thorn I think
of the thorn-covered God. I sit and listen.
An insect-wing is scratching the wall.
My wristwatch, ticking obstinately,
sends out a sound like a clenched
fist hammering and hammering.

In the yard a bony chicken
is picking at patches of sunlight.
Implements of the fields are going rusty
where the moist weather touched them.

Today we are submerged in the requiem
music of Good Friday.
The tree with its back turned to the house
is tranquil, as if it were dead.
Tomorrow
we'll be at each other's throats again.

CELTIC LANDSCAPE

I have passed through places of holiness
and witchcraft, rooms full of armour
preserved from the past.

A fine rain smudges the air
on hillsides worn smooth by pilgrim
and warrior. In cloister-ruins
congregations of grass worship the stars.
Stones and thistles hold down the horizon.

I am glad to find a world so different:
crags that are close to the next life,
a kingdom of lonesome animal tracks.

Bogcotton flutters making shadowy noise.
I see a cold sweat running down the mountains
and thorns in the sides of the ditches.

COMFORTER

She presses her breasts to streaming tears.
Once again she's a child's comforter

washing blood and dirt from scraped knees
or soothing a nervous imagination
awake at night in the silent house.

She is the story-teller, the water-carrier
who is never more serious than when she's looking
for a lost splinter in the palm of a hand

or turning the cool underside of a pillow
towards cheeks inflamed by childhood fevers.

MEMOIR

Matchlight set the mantled gas purring.
A kettle's breath climbed the wall.
The world I knew was spectral:
shadows grew from the dumb congregation
of coats in the hall.

From high windows
I heard the ragman calling
and barrels tumbling into cellars.
My eyes drank in the gliding funeral,
the feast day procession
 - a whole street coming to life
and quietening down.

On damp nights father rubbed on
ointment to ease his deep hurt.
I heard him: his audible shoeleather,
his chest full of phlegm.

In the ill-lit buildings
with water running through them
the voice of water crooned
in the cisterns.
Wardrobes, gasstoves, fusty parlours
smelled of the decades dead inside them.

CHILDHOOD

Elderberries ripe for picking
congregate at unreachable heights.

Down the lane, astray from the main roads,
it is like a place in the earliest folklore.
The walls of the tenantless house
are moribund. Neighbours know by divination
the weather of tomorrow.

With lungs full of straw
the scarecrow keeps vigil on what remains:
the stubble in the cornfield,
the traintrack pinned to the earth.

Older than the Old Testament
are the bones of the ravaged elm
 - the tree in the garden
mixing its roots with the roots of the homestead.

RICHARD KELL

Richard Kell was born in Co. Cork in 1927. After spending five years in India he was educated in Ireland. In 1983 he retired from his post as senior lecturer in English Literature to devote more time to creative work. He has published four books and three pamphlets of poems, has contributed to Irish and English periodicals, and has been represented in anthologies on both sides of the Atlantic. As a composer he has had pieces performed by several orchestras, chamber groups and soloists, both professional and amateur. In 1987 The Dedalus Press published Kell's new and selected poems, "In Praise of Warmth".

My admiration for several poets whose output has varied little in matter and form is tinged with envy. Now and then, having written a poem about some aspect of life that has particularly interested and moved me for many years, I have attempted similar poems in the hope of making a sequence or even a collection; but I have continued only when spontaneity, which is both compelling and liberating, hasn't been lost, and such occasions have been rare. I must accept myself, it seems, as a writer mainly of out-of-the-blue poems, wondering when the next poem is going to arrive, what it is going to say, and what shape it is going to have. (Even my poems in reverse rhyme, two of which are included here, have been written spontaneously; a few deliberate engagements with this exacting form ended in defeat. Not that spontaneity - or "inspiration" - implies absence of effort, but there's cold effort and warm effort). Of course I'd be delighted if some painstaking reader were to suggest that below the surface my work has unity.

My writing usually starts from an urgent awareness of a poem's content in general - from what I call an imaginative idea. The imagery - the sensory content - will sometimes be symbolic as well as, with or without metaphorical amplification, descriptive, and will often have a reflective or a meditative lining. I don't choose the verse form: it comes with the rhythms of phrases and sentences, and with shorter and longer runs of meaning, as the words are found - though obviously a shape that is to be repeated, for example that of a metred and rhymed couplet or stanza, reveals itself early, whereas a freeverse poem evolves unpredictably to the end. My style is on the whole fairly plain, but I hope it has phonic and imaginative resonance.

- Richard Kell

GOSPEL TOWN

Under its hump the town
endures nightfall. Sand
sweats as the tide uncovers
drainage and slimy stone.
Fairylights, fountain, bandstand
play the uneasy lovers.

Their ingrown hungers rage:
hot sermons, anodyne
of hymns, disturb the patter
of the hypnotist on the stage,
where tranced lips guzzle wine
from glasses filled with water.

Pure streams from granite ledges
fall through the glens, and swill
flat shingle solitudes
beyond the last bridges.
Unfathomably still
the black mountain broods.

SKY POEM

Taking off, he's glad of the rough power
  he has little use for: the towing plane
bullies both wind and spirit, but like a ripsaw
  slices along their grain.

At two thousand feet he drops the cable,
  feels the glider float free -
air sliding and whispering over wings
  like an ideal sea.

He plays off gravity against the surge of wind,
  moves the controls lightly to steer
uncalculated courses, true to the subtle
  weave of the atmosphere.

And knows the signs, the promises: where he sees
  a puff of cumulus he can soar
in slow circles on the rising heat.
  But nothing delights him more

than the unexpected gift of a blue thermal
  suddenly taking hold of the plane
in its long glide down, like a soft explosion
  urging it up again.

Sometimes, though, the sky turns sulky,
  withdraws her lithe and buoyant air:
the flier, for all his art, can only droop
  to a field in the middle of nowhere.

DEATH'S REPLY

I am not proud, nor do I seek dominion;
I do not destroy, or even sting.
Fire stings, and the nettle, and the scorpion;
violence breeds in every natural thing.

Innocent killers, you thrive on flesh or fruit;
guilty, you wreck and murder. You, not I,
sprang from the same imperishable root
as the wild energies of earth and sky.

Of the soul's destiny I know nothing;
but it may be, some part of you will thirst
for my Lethean purity, my soothing
emptiness, when life has done its worst.

THE GENTLEMAN WHO SNEAKED IN

Women! Persons! *Please!* Allow me to speak
just for a moment... Thank you... What I wanted
to say was this. To begin with, I understand.
No, I mean it: I do understand, and even
sympathize. In fact I'd go so far
as to call myself, with your permission of course,
a feminist. But there are, if I may say so,
feminists and feminists. Most of you here,
judging by what I've heard, would like to treat
men as they've treated women. I'm not surprised.
Age after grisly age of patriarchal
pride, insensitivity, exploitation -
no wonder you are militant! But consider:
has anything of enduring value ever
been gained by retaliation? Think, my friends!
Why would you take for model the sex you scorn?
Doing as they did, how would you help the world?
Cry out in protest, not in revenge and malice.
Firmly resist, but only in the name
of co-operation, sharing, mutual care,
equality, gentleness, all the lovely ways
that you can teach us now. We want to learn,
believe me. We *need* to learn if the human race
is not to... Thank you, ladies. Thanks for listening.
You're very kind... Thank you. I wish you well.

THE BUTTERFLY HEARS TCHAIKOVSKY

Did it blunder in from the street?
Worse, imagine it reborn
among the platform flowers,
the first venture of delicate wings
wafting it straight to hell.
Our minds flooded with metaphor -
Francesca, Paolo, the manic winds
they're whirled in, all music
out of a soul in torment -
we watch that silky flier
lost in the glare, bewildered by
the shock of storming brass.

Flickering, it soars, dips,
traverses, its frail career
scribbled on art in a real
violence. When the applause breaks
it's gone - twitching perhaps
beside a player's foot, finished off
by the tuba's final blast,
the sumptuous crash of gong and cymbals.

SABBATH TRIPTYCH

Music by Wagner: horns and violins
propose the condonation of his sins
who honoured God the Logos. Mr. Smith
would rather have a car to tinker with,
a hedge to trim, and God the Mechanist -
aloof, the cosmos ticking on his wrist.

Between the radio and electric shears,
myself and two Jehovah's Witnesses
contending on the doorstep. "It's all here
in black and white, the prophecies are clear"
they tell me, shaking dust off, snapping God
the Father in a briefcase. Overhead
the unclouded sunlight equably surveys
its colours redisposed a thousand ways.

THE LIFE OF BRIAN

Brian, employed in Saudi Arabia, favours
rigorous laws and the chopping off of hands,
but finds it a rewarding sideline
to sell illegal liquor.
Recounting which, I add with smug humility,
lifting a packet of Marlboro, "Of course
I can't throw stones: relying on these
is just as bad in a way."
"Worse," a friend obliges, and explains
with quiet authority that the land
cultivated by the tobacco barons
could have been used to feed the poor.
Right. And though he doesn't say so,
who but a hypocrite
would nod to his opinions while diffusing
a shifty veil of smoke?
Brian, frankly contemptuous of caring
for any but number one -
doing quite nicely money-wise,
enjoying far from his wife
a supply of emancipated nurses,
and keen, for his future security,
on the restoration of hanging
in the United Kingdom - puts me to shame.

Personal enterprise is more appealing
than indolent goodwill.
I'll shove my store of twenties
firmly into the dustbin, doing my bit
for the Third World, and rising
a notch or two in my friend's judgment.
Yes. Quite soon. When I'm feeling up to it.

PASTORAL

For years we've loved and trusted you
as teacher, manager, doctor, nurse
and all the rest. You were the flow
of life, even its deep source,
once the goddess with horned brow
who framed the pharaohs' universe.
Archaic stuff - yet, seeing you now
at the wheel, I like to think the bus
responds as plants and creatures do.
Proudly, over that unisex
no-nonsense kit of navy blue,
your hair still ripples long and loose.
You set me down where apples glow
and epitaphs are blurred with moss.

GOING FORWARD BACKWARDS

My favourite seat, beside the driver's cab,
was vacant, only this time at the back.
Objects a morning metro trip reveals -
the shiny rails, ruffled embankments, leaves
of tree and hedgerow, blood-red signal lights -
all flow away from me. In Hopi style,
its logic unassailable, I face
the vistas of the past; behind me, safe
against discovery, where the long track curls
towards a city's heart, the future lurks.

THE CHAIN OF BEING

Attracted by the fidget and the chirp,
a cat is eyeing a blackbird on his perch
deep in an apple tree. Her lifting tail
electrically writhes and flicks. Elate
with atavistic ravening, she walks
the paling like a rope, then, hooking claws
in bark, begins her stealthy climb. I know
the bird as if the garden were his own,
and he's the one I feel for. Why should pets,
now strangers to the jungle and the steppe,
be fondly understood when they attack
live meat as well as chunks of Kit-e-Kat?
Predictably, the feathered pal retires
by air, the furry one by land. All's right,
as Pippa sang - or is till panic tugs
compulsively at scores of tiny guts:
sharp cries attest a universal law,
the trees and bushes fill, and over all
except the Boeing miles above, where lips
are moist with mutton, peas, potato, Pils,
I see the hovering hawk, whose majesty
is founded on the humble kin he eats.

THIS BE THE CONVERSE

(After Larkin)

They buck you up, your mum and dad,
  Or if they don't they clearly should.
No decent parents let the bad
  They've handed on defeat the good.

Forebears you reckon daft old farts,
  Bucked up in their turn by a creed
Whose homely mixture warmed their hearts,
  Were just the counsellors you need.

Life is no continental shelf:
  It lifts and falls as mountains do.
So, if you have some kids yourself,
  They could reach higher ground than you.

CURRENTS

(i.m. Tony Baynes)

You showed me your poem mourning
a friend who floated down the Tyne;
told me during our only walk,
the kinked flood briefly lit by sun,
about those black twistings
that hurt your mind year after year.
Last night the news came
of your soaked body: now
I think of words, bridges,
deadly waters finally coupling.

MACDARA WOODS

Macdara Woods was born in Dublin in 1942. With Eiléan Ní Chuilleanáin, Leland Bardwell and Pearse Hutchinson, he is editor and founder of the literary magazine "Cyphers". He is a member of Aosdána, the Irish Artistic Academy. His poetry has been widely published and he has read from his work in several countries, including the U.S.A. In 1987 "Stopping the Lights in Ranelagh" was published by The Dedalus Press and in 1990 The Dedalus Press published his collection "The Hanged Man was not Surrendering".

A SEA OF ROOVES AND LEADED GABLES

A sea of rooves and leaded gables
made me feel easy in Paris
each in its way infamous as Casanova's
and each as much battened down; cone
upon cone in the morning, segmented,
opening on racy lines of washing;
on lives (Garlic and Gauloises climbing the air shaft
clearly misnomered a courtyard)
and the triangular shapes recede
becoming a morning-fluffed pigeon
or a blue boy whistling his way to decision —
the Lycée and rancour of leather.
The wine was good and the bread still better
though both remained from the night before;
hot coffee, cheese and apples on the parapet,
we hung like a bell in the frame of the building,
imaginary wings averted vertigo
and the curtains swung like a metronome.
In the night we flecked our eyes with sequins
and watched the yellow drops cascade
of Pernod poured in candle-light
and laughed and made love unafraid.
Waxlight wanes to morning; shapes remain
a brown ankle caught like a bird in the coverlet
an arm crooked lazily amain
two tangled bodies: les jeunes gens
en numero dix, Hôtel du Commerce
Rue de la Montagne Ste. Geneviève
and poems on the tiles like stains.
Trigonometry of course has rolled the bones —
would I at a distance know you again?
Not in mimosas, nor pine trees, nor bamboo,
not in the forests of the Ardennes
not on the geranium road to Alicante
not in the cornfield near Boulogne
not in the Berkshire haystacks we slept in
not by Dover Beach nor any ship's pitching.

In one place only perhaps I might find you
among walls and scree on the western seaboard
in the spray half blinded atop Dun Aengus
if your lips were salt and your smile were anxious
as under the willow you once smiled approval:
for it was not just time, love, that drove in the wedge.

THREE FIGURES IN A PUB WITH MUSIC

And since it has to be a pub scene faute de mieux
take one fat man spread upon a bar stool
talking of Billie Holliday's Strange Fruit
                                    Garrotted by the slit eyes
on his left he launches into relativity
Einstein he says was only his opinion
and don't ever - lifts glass - degenerate opinion
                                    The instruments
I admire the most are the trumpet and the voice
I don't Strange Fruit remember if the blacks were free
he lurches through an instantaneous high C

and slit eyes picks up faultless on the melody
O Mein Papa and Eddie Calvert was magnificent

                              His dexterous friend
the donkey-jacket-over-duck-egg-blue despite
initial difficulty in the depth of field
regains some clarity of tone and brain and pitch
                              (why am I so Black & Blue)
while slit eyes does a private quick-step to the jacks
and disappears the props and stools are switched
on absent friends the orchestra lights up the two
                              with martial music

81

for chat of history and politics and work and sex
and first name heads of state and drink and revolution
and melting dusty ice fills up the cracks

the dying notes
of Tipperary Far Away in Spanish Harlem

DAYS OF MAY 1985

for Niall

In the village street a stained-glass artist
Is trawling the shops for Brunswick black
On a morning when my mind is taken up with light
And light effects on silver halides

Or in Russells on a bleary Wednesday
Clients push in chafing and shooting their cuffs
Signalling pints but "spirits out first please"
Such are the limits of a year's horizons

This week brought Paul Durcan's postcard
With news of Robert Frost and mention of Mt. LaFayette
A catalogue of timber in New Hampshire
And yesterday my wife sailed in from Paris

To find me dressed again in campaign summer gear
Which doesn't differ much in truth from winter's
The addition or the stripping of a layer plus decorations
For my regimental Thursdays in the mad house

Being thus strappadoed I must have my story straight
And in my ley-lines find a bill of credence
Pick up on Leeson Street where I was born —
In the Appian Way my bones of childhood mock me

Yet these May mornings toiling to the Nursery
I sense my father's ghost in the wheeling migrant birds
And soon I can accept the electric invitation
Of my amazing son to the breathless world of cherry flowers.

THE COUNTRY OF BLOOD-RED FLOWERS

Looking out the window
six hours since I heard the Angelus
and there is no heavenly music
in the air above the house

Waiting for the dancer
to arrive across the fields tonight
with bag and bandages — a black
silk blindfold for my eyes

The window is unbarred
for locked cells may not be opened
where we find ourselves
in the country of blood-red flowers

Red flowers that bloom
at random in the chambers of the brain
along the blood
and lock into the mind and heart

She waits and she is right
little coelacanth — serpent brother
out there in the forest undergrowth
I hear her hesitate

Looking for patterns
she reformulates her steps -
again to the light of our lost rooms
love brings its own contagion

SANTA MARIA NOVELLA

This lonely angular man in railway stations
going home by cloud or wherever and travelling collapso
in the polish of Santa Maria Novella
drinking an orange juice and smoking a gauloise
he pauses mid-journey poised and folded at his table
warily by times and almost paternal
he eyes his Gucci-type metal executive briefcase
his sorcerer's link with home and substance
as if he has just been told it contains a time bomb
and his time has ticked its hour up

Nor is he any too sure of these foreign coins
and he lays them out on his palm at intervals
to inspect them and survey them into sense
and all unbeknownst to him his eyebrows creep up
his head twitches to the side and his eyes widen
as he talks to the coins giving them instruction
and his other angular hand unships itself
an admonitory digit wagging up and down
until it anchors in under his chin
and he returns to the station self-service Ristorante
wondering if we have noticed his temporary absence

But we are all at odds here quartered off
set apart behind a bright green rope

I am considering the kilo of garlic in my bag
its oils and its fine rich weight and aroma
and this Florentine heat and I'm wondering
if my fellow passengers on the night train to Paris
will appreciate my addition to their journey
and all unbeknownst to myself
I have lifted the plastic bag to my head inhaling
as if to clear a lifetime of asthma
bursting my lungs with the must of garlic
I am tunnelling beneath the platforms of Florence
fiercely with my eyes shut
crushing wild garlic on the walls of my sett

Among the reflections and marble of Santa Maria Novella
magic samurai are sheathing magic cameras
a waiter slides by on velvet skates
an elderly German hitches up his shorts
the cool service area pauses unexpectantly
— again nothing has happened —
and the catch of the station clock flips over

IN THE RANELAGH GARDENS:
EASTER SATURDAY 1988

Easter falls early this year
at the end of a mild winter —
tomorrow the sun will dance on the ceiling
at midnight on Thursday by the sea I heard
Summer rustling in the palms

Listen said the voice
for years I have been fighting my way up out of this
climbing out of this black hole
pushing past the bog oak
and this black weight that hugs my rib cage

On a street corner in Rome my brother-in-law
the Guardian of Paradise reflects
Arabian gentleman in camel hair
how can I have grown so old he says
staring into his daughter's camera lens

I thought of him again last night
and looked for design in our ad hoc lives
breathing cool air from the surface of the pond
remembering I must not be in competition
not even with myself

Listen said the voice
for years I have been in the shallows of this lake
a creature of the reeds
hunting under drowned and folded leaves
with the water beetles

SCORPIONS

I built a castello of stones and mud
and great baulks of seasoned timber
with oak doors in the walls
and then I whitewashed the walls on the inside
put a fire-back and pots in the fire-place
a new-forged crane and hooks and chain

and in preparation for the siege ahead
I laid in logs and charcoal
onions and oil and garlic
and sides of bacon hanging from the beams
and then I sat back and waited
this whole peninsula was waiting
and I was European and waiting for the Barbarians

That German tonight in Castiglione del Lago
drunk lifted up a woman's dress
his companion night-jars screeching in the dark
pesca di mare pesca di mare
laughing their way up the cobbled street
pesca di mare pesce di mare
her curved gold abdomen a peach?
And in Panicale yesterday another
a madman torched himself and teenage son
we heard the ambulance climb screaming up the hill
the Corriere dell' Umbria in hot pursuit
and I thought of WeeGee
WeeGee flashing through the New York night
shadowing death for the Saturday Post
and I was European and waiting for the Barbarians

And in the end like dreams they came
black scorpions came down my walls to join me
finding recognition in the whites of my eyes
soot creatures from before my childhood
from that rain-streaked chimney space
black scorpions came down my white wash walls
and I know the limits of this farm-house hearth
what people occupied this place
my grandmother's bedroom stretching away
away from the house and the hill and the furze
my dead uncles standing like frozen horses
and the beasts that stamp and knock beneath
and I am European and waiting for the Barbarians

THE BANKS OF THE DANUBE

(after the Dordán concert in Butler House,
    Kilkenny, January 1991)

In another City nearly fifty
and that slow air tears my lungs
ageing backlit figure
in the shadows out of focus
some dark night outside
and time stops still — I am
the floating isolated skull
over there in the smoky corner
the faded picture on the poster
fallen down behind the till
still looking out for love

Cold and listening to music
slow air and punctured lungs
plans shelved again and
folded up in Rand McNally
that woman in Chicago
who slept with a loaded gun —
have I somehow outlived them all
the lovers and the drunks
and all my dispossessed
my own poor lost hussars at one
with moonlight and blue music

Music in the air tonight
that slow air tears my lungs
and women comb the killing fields
to find dead lovers news of men
stretched naked in the streets
so cold so white as ice tonight
beneath the Precinct wall
along the levee and the slips
on the river-walks and quays
by this salt fatal river —
this landlocked frozen sea

Trapped until Winter cracks
in the ice outside your door
tomorrow morning I will ask —
St Bridgid's Day the first of Spring —
which road to take to catch
my nineteen-forties distant self
walking in unfamiliar snow
the sting of sea foam in my mouth
rock salt in the fields — tonight
this same slow air is yours
this slow air fills the room

LES CÔTES DU TENNESSEE

The colours you will walk in little son
these countries that are yours were mine
were magical and strange such contradictions
the space bat angel spread its wings
and came down burning from the sun —
are magical and strange and dangerous
and oh the world is full of crooks and heroes
beware the cargo when your ship comes in
the autumn serpent in the stubble field
those hungry spiders in our dusty rooms
have registered and taken note
they hold our image in their thousand eyes

Forty one years later the tune still plays
through this April afternoon my birthday
in the skies above the Lost River Ranch
Highway 76 and the Mississippi delta
Les Côtes du Tennessee and *Beausoleil*
the space bat dragon loops and sings
make me an angel that flies from Montgomery
make me a poster of an old rodeo
just give me one thing that I can hold on to
and the world is full of crooks and heroes —
I have been listening since East Liberty
since West Palm Beach and since the dawn

Vrai Citoyen du Monde of all the dawns
alone or shared in empty rooms
or standing by a ship's rail watching
this self-same Mississippi sun come up
down East of Wexford and the Tuskar Rock
in flight from time and circumstance — at
thirty thousand feet above pretence we start
to drop for Arkansas and South Missouri
new rooms new names new answers friends
as the space bat angel dragon sings
in a world made right for crooks and heroes
that if defeated we fly down in flames

90

HUGH MAXTON

Hugh Maxton was born outside Aughrim, Co Wicklow, in 1947. He is well known as critic and literary historian, and is a member of Aosdána. He has translated a selection of the poetry of the Hungarian poet Agnes Nemes Nagy, "Between", published in 1988 by Corvina Press, Budapest and The Dedalus Press, Dublin. In 1991 The Dedalus Press published his new and selected poems, "The Engraved Passion." Hugh Maxton lives in Dublin.

Expressed in historical terms, the problem of the contemporary Irish poet is this - how to inherit, enjoy, and dispose of a modernism that never quite existed. Or in moral terms - How should he or she, or simply I, respond to a degree of violence too petty for registration in the world's eyes, too gross for the contemplative gaze, and always too continuously discrete and temporary to be seized and absorbed?

I began in the late 1960s, by writing love poems about megalithic monuments. History remains of course, and I detect a strain of puritan animus directed against passion. Poetry is a fire, well banked-down that it may warm survivors on the even-colder nights to come.

The poems selected here might be referred to recent events. "Nocturne" was written in Derry in late 1971, and readers may want to know my father died in 1961 - another poem says so. "De Profundis" and "Ode" are a little later, taking Nature as only our second nature. "Deutschland" carries its own date-line: eleven years after Bloody Sunday, the aniversary fell on a Sunday (as if in mimicry of Yeats's platonic years.) "Cloud" was written after I watched on television bags of people recovered from a bombed disco, *circa* 1982.

The scene shifts, but not away. The institution alluded to in "At the Protestant Museum" may be found on Engels Tér, Budapest, though the street-name may have changed by the time you get there. The sequence was written in early 1983 during a period of deep isolation and remaking. "Bukharin's Fox", 1989, is written in a syllabic metre of my own devising, with acknowledgements to early Gaelic literature. "The Star of Kilmainham" owes something to the satiric example of Austin Clarke; it's the work of a local complainer who fears that God's eye has been wiped.

- Hugh Maxton

ODE

To read our few poets
you'd think there had been
a recent withdrawal
from the land of the stoat
and the yellow-scarf mouse;

a land in which nothing
twitches in the woodlands
but our nerves,
and every swan
is someone else's daughter.

Their lives are mashed
in the engine of politics
or, high on dynamite,
they industrialise the old dreads.
Yet truth is

ours is still a rural country.
In which we never need
the stoat for savagery
or the yellow-scarf
for extinction.

NOCTURNE

Night on the accustomed
roadway draws past;
commercial mottoes
hidden in its plush,

ancestral fragments
launched on the lost
kinetic fears
the hours conjure.

Tiny instances of war
sound alone,
and the barometer
draws itself upright.

In the morning
the usual rubbish
falls from my bowels;
I smell of my father.

DE PROFUNDIS

The fossil-fish is pale; we mined this pair
just forty minutes out from the hotel.
We thought it deader than the dinosaur,
a pattern in stone, an empty cell-
ular abstraction. Which proved an error.
Below the dreaming tropic lies a chill
region flattened by thirty gravities;
and water there is thicker than blood,
small and lucid as a lens which is
the sum of what it sees. History's rude
moralities are rammed down on us,
the teething beasts that we live among.

We rise with bursting bodies and confound
the placid statisticians on the ground.

DEUTSCHLAND

The Minority always guilty: (Louis MacNeice)
                    The thing not done,
                    thing considered slowly
                    as a word and chosen
                    as itself the act
                    of notcommitting
                    the atrocity.

                    It was eleven years ago.
                    Admonished now
                    by the one body among them
                    whom I love.

                    To have been there
                    at the back of the crowd
                    an adequate memory.

Clarity's no
aide-memoire:
the cold field
lay between the houses
like a natural misunderstanding.
The club that night
sound dead.

These nights are endless,
remembering and retelling
we forge ourselves and sorrows,
a thousand
recitations of identity.
How we become
our culled inheritors,

divided between shrill
unspoken research
granite emotion,
between these -
containment of hysteria
retaliation's exile.

Eleven years now,
these nights are endless,
an adequate memory.
We forget ourselves and sorrows.
And start at the thing not done,
the atrocity.

Sunday 30.1.83

CLOUD

Invisible mountain.
White eye of the self.
Look at the screen
regard my death.

In the harbour mouth
a blacknecked grebe.
On the mountain
invisible cloud.

And from day to day.
A psychology of
exploded moments
falls.

It is true
the blacknecked grebe
fishes quite
like no other.

It is true
the species
manifests no
little identity.

A language
without agreement.
Voice and limb
blown.

Eye hanging a fob.
Invisible mountain
in the harbourmouth.
Regard my death.

AT THE PROTESTANT MUSEUM

1. I'm getting used to not understanding.
Underpasses chorus my migration.
Words turn to music on the landing
by my room and pantry, my exotic ration.

Enough is riches. Rare beef and cabbage
translated gravely on learned menus
I take and eat. On average

96

I list necessity with the virtues.

Mild days mounting to become January;
the feminine rhymes distress
a calendar at once full and free.
Time passes to make the future less.

Hus and Melanchton and Luther
thumbed the pages of my testing youth.
We hardly knew them, and yet thought them blessed.
And were the chosen of a king's protest.

The kiss of privilege, favours of the poor;
jokes we could afford, all this and more
we managed faithfully. We did not hear
a travelling preacher's echo - 'history stops here.'

> 2.   'I, Dr Luther, declare
> that to my dear
> and faithful wife Kate,
> for her own support
> or (as is usual)
> for her entire use and disposal
> I bequeath firstly:
> a small propetry
> at Fulsdorf
> which I bought and restored ...
>
> I have not used
> legal expression
> (and for good reason)
> I really am
> namely under heaven
> and earth and even in hell,
> a well-known, just
> and respected judge
> whose word no
> notary profiscal
> will budge.'

3. This is the testimony of the pastor-lieutenant:

'He asked me to go to his wife when the situation improves, and tell her to have his corpse exhumed for burial at Tarpa in the Calvinist cemetery, there being no Lutheran.

He asked me for some alcohol. He mixed wine from the chalice with brandy a soldier brought. And he drank it.

Then he had diarrhoea, and asked me to leave him by himself. - Some minutes later, he asked me to come in again. He asked me to give an account of his last hours to his wife. At that, the soldier faltered and kissed the hand of Bajcsy-Zsilinszky.

Only after it was over was I ordered to the place of execution. I wasn't allowed to bless his ashes as he was taken for burial.'

> **4.** History stops here.
> The curator wipes up the takings
> and closes the shop,
> goes home and lights the stove,
> smiles in the mirror
> with unsuspected gold.
> She is a treasure,
> she is a treasure of the Lord.
>
> History stops here.
> In a back-flip the mind
> reverts home
> to the sheds and attics,
> power drills,
> and farm buildings.
> Security, the home rules,
> the years of promise,
> the power drills,
> the secret police of majesty's
> Parachute Regiment
> under the chairmanship of the lord
> Widgery. *Fidei defensor;*
> retain the tongue

proclaimed, pack the museums.

History stops here,
with the retrospective
muse of parliament.
The favours of the poor,
mild day with neighbours.

5. Prepared now to stop in the Metro
I pray at your station. Bajcsy-Zsilinszky.
Strangeness abates strangeness, can undo
pride that speaks of death with dignity.

An abstracted sceptic weeping red tears,
caught the distance between word and image,
caught in the schism between home and fear,
caught up in the mere oneness of an age.

*

Pray for the soul of Bajcsy-Zsilinszky.
Pray for the soul of Lieutenant Shepherd.
Pray for the soul of Hunter Gowan who a week prior to the late
insurrection cut with his sword the finger off a papish to whisk
his punch as true huntsmen do with the fox's brush.
Pray for the soul of Christ in whom all things begin.

BUKHARIN'S FOX

1. At Leningrad terminal
the undercarriage clattered
on the tarmac like the huge
claws of an arctic eagle
a metre short of its prey.

A fox turned blandly to go.
The birch that shadow themselves
with bruised growth stood open
on the edge of the airport -
the emigrés, the accused.

Can the Truth cease to be true?
Better - how long does it take
for demon or beast to die
reaching his old, iced-up haunts?
And Nature, does it close ranks

when the word barely goes out
annulling the enterprise?
Dialectic and divorce,
he had known each to be shrewd
visiting madame Stalin.

2. Pavlov called again, amazed
at my commissar's grasp of
biology. His lectures
were based on research commenced
when I was just eleven.

Osip's brother has been lifted.
Poet and wife have me plagued.
He thinks Gorky's not gifted,
has slapped Tolstoy in the bake.
Brother, I pray, save thyself.

Remember, Koba, the arm-
wrestling, the falls and throws
when we were young and comrades?
I won by means of my height.
Shortly, I am in the throes.

Your wife? Put this posthumous
note in the drawer with Lenin's
crisp rebuke of your pawing
his missus. I suppose mine
can with-stand another death.

3. A wisp of smoke rose from the box
hiding the same hands. The court
took note of the confessions,
and Rosengolts breaking down

into daft unfinished song.

On the day no documents
existed. The accused were
the competent witnesses.
By the year's end, a poet
who mocked the gunman's stubby

fingers died naturally.
How the truth rang hollowly,
how the prisoner returned
each question as its answer,
how the song swallowed itself

as a beast enters its lair.
Beast and truth, nature and lair,
one slips into the other.
Vomit and motiv - please
choose, quickly enter your pleas.

4. In the Taynitsky Gardens
after he ceased to exist
the grass annually hardens
and forgives like the tourists
with their guilt-ridden questions.

Memoirs of Koba's daughter
speak of the gods and the good
as if the one might pardon
the other party without
snorts of demonic laughter.

The guides so-call Government
Hotel where some two per cent
of the nomenklatura
survived intact the era
with only a loss of face.

Gold leaf, red square, black market.
The dealers have adjusted

to the rues of history
and its leavings, to point out
the detachment of soldiers.

5.   Three times the beast to its lair,
I returned to my office.
Three times my gun in my mouth,
Lenin turned to his statue.
The engines race to reverse.

He loved a crippled hawk caged.
Adders sunned themselves in jars,
frogs, hedgehogs, and Pavlov's dogs.
Spring, and summer, then the fall.
Nature has its own career.

For the best part of six months
I, Anna Larina, stood
in iced-water, warming it
with piss and menstrual blood.
Then released into the camps

for another eighteen years.
Meanwhile the fox hid and sought
in the Taynitsky Gardens
throughout the long war with naught
but monuments for comfort.

THE STAR OF KILMAINHAM

At the reception of Christ J. Herod,
Angels stood guard in Bully's Acre,
The Great Book held aloft by Theo for God
As the prophets dropped below their maker.

Turning a new leaf each tomorrow
No sinner's too big for intervention.
Icarus falls? Let him drown or row
In with a crowd he'd vomit to mention.

28.12.'91

102

TOM MAC INTYRE

Tom Mac Intyre was born in Cavan. He is one of Ireland's best-known playrights; his plays include <u>The Great Hunger,</u> <u>Rise up Lovely Sweeney,</u> <u>Dance for Your Daddy</u> and <u>Kitty O'Shea</u>. He has been awarded bursaries from the Arts Council and in 1981 he became a member of Aosdána. In 1987 The Dedalus Press published his collection of poems, *I Bailed out at Ardee* and in 1990 his most recent collection, *Fleurs-Du-Lit.*

We'd set out for our ramble. The ostensible purpose was to find the turkeys but, truth was, she flourished most in the dusk, and knew it. This was the hour in which she took possession of the landscape, and, same motion, introduced it to me.

Dusk melting the hills, bringing in the lakes, we'd leave the lane and take to the fields. There was never much talk, the odd crow active, shout of a blackbird. She'd always make for a particular *plantin'* - a stand of fir boldly positioned in mid-meadow. A wayward wall circled it. All colours of the day this place spoke strangeness. In the dusk it seethed.

The *plantin'* watched us coming, agreed with that, made us at home. It knew our deep intent - to do nothing at all. We'd stand in the lee of the timber and allow the evening approach. Stir in the firs - far-away stir, whistle of a bat, Sheridan's scattered dog. There were times we lingered for the first stars.

Eventually, the turkeys would interrupt our reverie. We'd process back to the house, the flock chirruping, stretching their necks as we hit the lane.

Look at the moon back on her heel - I hear her - *What's that a sign of?*

Shut that gate. Say good-night to the *plantin'* - stranger, and close relation, that watched us going, agreed with that, would be there tomorrow, all the tomorrows, and the day after.

-Tom Mac Intyre

CONNEMARA

A mighty number -

So conversable the mountains -
Shore patient as an insect -
The heave always from the west -

Any given view worth two meals a day -

(Don't go to sleep in a bog -
Don't go to sea without a stone on the floor of the boat -
Don't go puttin' your arms around the world -)

Place to fall in love again, pillage round-sticks, put wheels
on crabs, save for the six o'clock news -

The conger, with mane,
wrapped three times
'round the canoe,

sentry wild-goose
torn to bits
for slack on the job,

from the turn of the day
the step of the cock
one inch longer -

Most things come by threes -

Rock where the butterfly rests -
Rumours between foam and water -
Wise ashes, plunge your hand.

Where there's muck there's luck.

And what else?

The top of the tide -
The spoon of the breast -

The women Gale Force Nine -
The men Oriental in the *bearna baol* -

And the islands, the islands, I touched them, *a gradh gheal*,
islands like cats on the warm morning rug of the sea...

CHILD

Often he wears my son's face,
seizes me as of right,
takes me the unused path
to the green gate,

how ripe the leaves,
my fingers touch vines,
the vines grip iron.

Naked in the field,
shoulders like a bull-calf,
he pucks the ball ten times
the length within my compass.

I've tried to kill him,

I've seen the digger
dripping mud and stones
hold up his broken shape,

week later met him
healthy as a frog,

untouched, unchanged,
my breath, my clay,
my open hand

FATHER

My shoulder knows his coffin
best of all, I was
the one who wasn't there.

Nightly, a bell calls,
I rise, hunt a funeral,
stumble home.

      Once though,
he stood before me,
spade outstretched,
spun handle, blade,
found a radius, three times
fed ordered circles
into my secret breath,

put the spade aside,
touched my face -

Short sorrow is a long sword -

those were his words,

then the light
was customary gray.

RETURN VISIT

There's a sign,
you that's one for signs,

you've climbed the mountain,
gone into the wood
to touch the stones -

the stones can't be found.

Scan the view.
Weigh the lean
mid-winter air.

That sapper's mark
has its eye on me.

I stand there years,

know-nothing,
let my feet call,
Shantemon wraps me,
the tart shade goes
down like sweet milk,
rib-root, rib-rock,

briar's grip,
bark-lice,
sacral shaft.

I've lived here years.

Five stones
divide the trees.

Pick your step now
in the good quiet,
enter the old
enclosure,

how they wait,
wait and move,
light along their shoulders
the underside of light,
this season's word
and sumptuary kiss.

Bathe in that light.
Give them your hand.

THE PURPLE FLOWER

The purple flower
sprig of a thing
finding a way

the purple yields
underplumage
first feathering's
indolent down

the purple frees
purple on fire
tourbillon deeps
fire the purple

the petals move
five to the flower
as one they move
pillow and fire
one in the weave

listen and hear
hear to the far
end of your bones

PRESTISSIMO

Gram for gram
no wilder-looking
specimen abroad,

the hooked beak,
the orange eye,
that barred breast,

holding you down
those talons drive
the hard bargain,

"I'm heir-presumptive",
he's always told you,
"to your presumptions",

the beak whirrs,
knows it's not
for stirring tea
he has it,

eye fulsome now,
the breast - perpends,
"Table d'hôte or
à la carte?" "Buffet" -
did he hear you say?

you've got to like him,
see to his needs,

smile as he feeds
without bothering to kill.

OCTOBER MORNING

Hussy vermilion rose-hip,
haw's *Beaujolais Nouveau,*

blackberry's puckered regret,
comether drowse of the sloe,

snowberry's clustered
pallor on pallor,

fistfuls of silence
where winter winds blow.

REVERSE CHARGES

You should have known Eve,
the girl next door, fair
priestess of *vin ordinaire*,

or what about Helen?
patchouli of boudoir, poetry
talk, arc of her lingerie
a Calder mobile, *Helen*,
that was the rainy season,

I was born for Mary's
multiple assumptions, annunciations,
Mary, mine ethereal Mary,
come back Eve from Tipperary,

which brings us to Sophie,
Sophie, where are you?
and why don't you call?

oh, Eve on a journey,
Helen turned wise, Mary
down from the mountain,

I wait by the phone,

Sophie, please call. Call,
Sophie. Sophie, please call.

CHANGING HOUSE

Last chest, last drawer,
a lock of woman's hair.
Her very colour, sheen,
blonde brought up on sun.

Test the strands, brittle
something, sapless, stagey.
Smell, as you often did,
gulp now, gulp your fill.
Sandalwood of the drawer.

Look at it again,
light on your palm.

Finders -
Keepers -
Losers.

Soundlessly, the plastic bag
takes it in one go.

THE SEA POTATO

My love brings
a sea potato, heart
urchin of the lower shore,
modestly sand-coloured
with soft backward-
pointing spines: no teeth,
she asserts, who has well
perused her *objet trouvé*,
the versatile spines pass food
to the pert mouth,
and, she is not slow
to point out the sea
potato is singularly petalled,
her pliant index finger
explores, reveals, five
dorsal petals, anterior
extending a sibilant
auxiliary mouthward groove -
Smell, she says: fume,
fume of salt furrows,

Listen, she says, places
against my ear the soft
sand-coloured thing:

arpeggio, silken, ten
thousand shells chime
in the wave's undertow.

AISLING GEAL

The one-strand river
never looked better,
pleasure-bound
the coral cove,
the quiet's in love,

away to the right
two pup seals dandle
slack of the tide,
breast-to-breast splash
each other, all comers,
jap me with beginning,
middle, end, shout --

Fall into the milk
and spend your luck.
The night will come
you'll give us suck.

A beat. Centuries.
I find a whisper,
the whisper carries
life and limb --

Yours be mine
the time to play.
Mine be yours
the time to swim.

MANY WHILE PLAYING

Europa, Persephone,
had no need
of amphetamines,

some for flowers,
more for curls,
spill your pearls,
eat the world --

oh, the bagel-babies
of my salad days
and green enjambments --

let's gather bog-myrtle,
doss above on the hill,
and, Wistful, heed well,

if you don't see a star-wheel,
the star-wheels shine still.

DENNIS O'DRISCOLL

Dennis O'Driscoll was born in Thurles, Co. Tipperary, in 1954. He has reviewed poetry regularly for Irish and English papers and magazines. He works in Dublin. He has published two collections of poetry; "*Kist*" appeared from the Dolmen Press in 1982; and "*Hidden Extras*" was published in 1987 by Anvil Press Poetry, London, and The Dedalus Press.

Silence is the source and destination of poetry. A poem's conception should be spontaneous, though labour may be difficult.

***

Writing is surprisingly non-cumulative. One poem is not succeeded automatically by a more mature one. Each generation is not more skilled than the one before.

***

Poetry is bread for starving language; too often, it is permitted to eat cake.

***

What I would wish for is that kind of personal language into which everything can be translated imaginatively, so that no experience is without poetic potential - Stephen Dobyns, Roy Fuller, James Schuyler, Peter Reading, Norman MacCaig, Fleur Adcock, Seamus Heaney and Thomas Kinsella are among the contemporary poets to have reached this perfect pitch.

***

The time available to me for poetry after a day at the office is like a tiny profit margin I must work within. Take any of it away and I am at a total loss.

***

Poetry rather than fiction is the most appropriate form for those of us whose existences are as uneventful as they are routine but who find that the full force of life can be felt in a sheltered room.

***

A poet must try to put an accurate price-tag on life without either borrowing or inflating language.

***

I write with my back to a wall supporting shelves of the major poets. To face them would be to face an unpalatable truth - that one's chances of joining them are exceedingly remote.

***

Some revision is as direct and uncomplicated as plucking a loose thread from a new jacket. Often, however, one makes the depressing discovery that the whole fabric has begun to unravel with that single pluck and the material proves much less serviceable than had been imagined.

***

I have a big wickerwork waste-paper basket. It's in place under my desk. *Here's to the poems of the future!*

- Dennis O'Driscoll

G-PLAN ANGST

He has everything.
A beautiful young wife.
A comfortable home.
A secure job.
A velvet three-piece suite.
A metallic-silver car.
A mahogany cocktail cabinet.
A rugby trophy.
A remote-controlled music centre.
A set of golf clubs under the hallstand.
A fair-haired daughter learning to walk.

What he is afraid of most
and what keeps him tossing some nights
on the electric underblanket,
listening to the antique clock
clicking as if with disapproval from the landing,
are the stories that begin:
He had everything.
A beautiful young wife.
A comfortable home.
A secure job.
Then one day.

HERE AND NOW

There's a mirror that has seen me
for the last time - Borges

There are poems I could write only in the present tense
that I will never be in a position to again:
about looking into a mirror and seeing not one grey hair
or sitting with you in an unburgled living room,
the terminal diseases still dormant in our cells.

Or there is the poem of this very moment,
sunset streaking the horizon like a circus poster,
the sky wearing a v-neck of homing geese,
bubbles of fleece blowing from dandelion and thistle,
a wasp in jockey colours racing the dark.

There is the poem of this unrecorded second,
so nondescript, so tame, so plain:
the smack of a gardener's spade, a distracting hum,
radio jingles leaching through a parked car;
and now a milkman's helper is distributing bills.

Somewhere else, locked in our past tense, beyond grasp,
first lovers thrill to mutual discoveries
— beginnings we too recall, pristine invigorating dawns
fresh as if earth's architect just left,
cloud's mortar setting above building-rubble hills.

And elsewhere, too, a world of frenzy: commodity markets,
blackberry riot police, crises of age and youth.
The unwrinkled glass that holds me in the balance
between past and future is a river I must cross,
floating out of depth towards its unreflective side.

REPUBLICAN SYMPATHIES

What I have always liked about the Irish Republic
is that it is, of all the societies that I know,
the least 'sexy' — Donald Davie

It is always raining on this bleak country.
Windows in their rustproof frames are never silent.
Our cottages are damp-proofed to no avail.
Bruise marks of mould deface wallpaper skin.
Smells of decay assail us in our musty sitting-rooms.

How could sexiness survive this purifying climate?
Where would cut-away shoes, see-through blouses,
figure-hugging mini-skirts fit into this arthritic scheme?
Chunky-knits and padded anoraks are the order of the day;
hot-water bottles, flannel bedwear make nights sensuous.

Somewhere, annually, Miss Ireland is announced
and shivers in ciré swimwear just long enough
for ogling lenses to record her nerve.
Occasionally, too, fishnets and high heels are glimpsed,
springing across a bus-stop flood ...

Forecasts are seldom good here, bringing forebodings
of worse weather, deteriorating trade, added unemployment.
Days are so dark the end of the world never appears far off.
Hay floats, unharvested, in flooded fields.
The beauty of this land lies mostly in reflection.

Our birth rate stays high (boredom, Vatican encyclicals?):
erotic signals are given off, it seems — muffled
behind layers of ribbed woollen tights, thermal underwear.
What need have we of sex shops, contraceptives?
Yielding Sile na Gigs are cut down to size by an East wind;

summer is a few golden straws to grasp on between showers.

OFFICE PHOTOGRAPH

for Margaret O'Sullivan

There will be no reunion for this class of people:
some are dead already; one immured in a convent;
others ill, retired, transferred, settled abroad.

But, for the duration of this photograph,
a fresh, foot-stamping morning reigns
(a few wear overcoats) and in the foreground

a wiry tree is barbed with buds.
Behind us, sun disperses shadows
of venetian blinds, like prison bars, on desks

and projects the film of dust specks
fidgeting on our stacked backlog of files.
We stare, smiling and clear-eyed, into a pensionable future.

Dressed in our best and at companionable ease,
we stand oblivious of how such scenes
will flash before us, recalling features

out of memory's frame, blurred by moving time;
and how this tableau, so tranquil in spring light,
so fixed in a known hour and place,

will develop into a focal point of change
as news comes of some name we match, then,
to a placid, frank, unwary face.

THURLES

after Zbigniew Herbert

A childhood too boring for words
is lost without a fragment in that town.
And, so, I have held my tongue about its gutturals;
its sky slated consistently with cloud;
its mossy roofs restraining excesses of rain.

One house watches out for me, though.
I know where its cabbage colander is kept
and the special knack required to use its tin-opener
and the exact key in which the kitchen door,
scuffed by a ring-board, creaks:

things I cannot depict in dictionary terms,
through heartless words that fail to resonate.
Others are suppressed in embarrassment or pain
(all families have passed their own equivalents
to the Official Secrets Act).

Yet everything there translates into feeling:
the plates the dead have eaten from before us,
the layers of wallpaper that still pattern memory,
the hairline crack in marble that was my fault,
the rose-arched garden explored down to its last stone.

Back in the city, I resort to standard words again.
Unable to identify possessions by their first names,
I call them only by their surnames
— by their brand names —
and will never discover their real names.

NORMALLY SPEAKING

To assume everything has meaning.
To return at evening
feeling you have earned a rest
and put your feet up
before a glowing TV set and fire.
To have your favourite shows.
To be married to a local
whom your parents absolutely adore.
To be satisfied with what you have,
the neighbours, the current hemline,
the dual immersion, the government doing its best.
To keep to an average size
and buy clothes off the rack.
To bear the kind of face

that can be made-up to prettiness.
To head contentedly for work
knowing how bored you'd be at home.
To book holidays to where bodies blend,
tanned like sandgrains.
To be given to little excesses,
Christmas hangovers, spike high heels,
chocolate eclair binges, lightened hair.
To postpone children until the house extension
can be afforded and the car paid off.
To see the world through double glazing
and find nothing wrong.
To expect to go on living like this
and to look straight forward. No regrets.
To get up each day neither in wonder nor in fear,
meeting people on the bus you recognise
and who accept you, without question, for what you are.

DAY AND NIGHT

1
wrapped in a sheer white negligée
    you are a fog-bound landscape
familiar but seen in a new light
    transformed by seamless mist
tantalising, trimmed with tufts of cloud
    I know that after the fog lifts
all will be sultry and warm
    I can detect a sun-like breast
already radiating through the nylon dawn

2
in hot darkness, the transistor on
    a five-note raga plays
five senses that ascend the scale of longing:
    until the gasps of music peter out
and a taut night is plucked limp
    we are out of meaning's reach
your vellum blotted with invisible ink
    my head at rest
between your breasts' parentheses

SPOILED CHILD

my child recedes inside me
and need never puzzle where it came from
or lose a football in the dusty laurel bushes
or sneak change from my jacket to buy sweets

my child will not engage in active military service
or make excuses about its school report
or look up from a picture book, dribbling a pink smile
or qualify for free glasses or school lunch

my child will not become a prodigy of musicianship or crime
and will evince no appetite for hamburgers or drugs
and will suffer neither orgasm nor kidney stones
reduced neither to a statistic nor a sacrifice

my child will not play space games with its cousins
or sit adrift on a grandparent's lap
or slit its wrists or erect a loving headstone on my grave
or store a secret name for frogs or treetops

my child will not be a comfort to my old age
my child will not be cheated or promoted or denied
my child will trail me, like a guardian angel, all my life
its blemishes, its beauty, its shortcomings and its promise

forever unsullied and unfulfilled

WAY OF LIFE

The longest queues.
The cheapest cuts.

The high season beaches.
The rush hour delays.

The densely-populated quarters.
The comprehensive schools.

The public ward for babies.
The public house for celebration.

The special offers.
The soccer turnstiles.

When admission was reduced.
When group rates were available.

During lunchtime or weekend.
During Sunday or bank holiday.

At weddings, parks, parades.
At Christmas markets, January sales.

Wherever people gathered.
When crowds took to the streets.

DISARMAMENT

your first grey hairs
are plucked out readily enough
and harmony restored

that metal sheen proliferates
and you rish baldness
as you eliminate invaders

MISTAKEN IDENTITY

Could I begin by asking what you were thinking of as the gunman approached?

Nothing very precise, actually. I was vaguely annoyed at pet
owners. It's not fair to those who have to walk the streets. I'm
nearly sure I had a flash of memory also — something had re-
minded me of the nest under the yew at my grandmother's. We
found a clutch of warm, fawn eggs one summer there. A girl,
too, I think, a belt tied loosely round her waist?

Yes, that's right. She proved to be a key witness.

I've just recalled the way the hens would tap their legs like tun-
ing forks, then hold their drawling notes long into the afternoon.
My grandmother was always making clothes — knitting or
crochet. Or baking. A riot of peach flans and seed cakes and rasp-
berry meringues.

What kind of fear did you have as the killer was about to strike?

I was a bit behind in my work. A few times in the last year or so
a pain had flared down my left thigh. Fear that anything would
happen to the family, that Jim would go near the quarry again.
That the new video would be robbed during our holiday.

Can you describe how you felt after you learned the news?

It was a kind of reverse dream. You know how when you dream of having done something with someone (or *to* someone, as it often is) you expect them to remember the experience too. I once flew under the waves with the kids, viewing candy-striped fish from the cabin ... This time, it is they who have all the details and I don't remember any of it — the shot, the emulsion of blood, the surgeon, the dizzy lowering into the clay, the statement about mistaken identity.

What would you like to have one more glimpse of?

The family, of course. My record rack. A girl in tennis dress. A sky aerated with stars. Swallows in summer that pedal uphill, then freewheel down. A blackbird on my front lawn charming worms. Sparks of moonlight kindling a tree. More ordinary things — the Sunday lunch just after it is served, the steaming gold of roast potatoes and chicken skin. The sheets folded after ironing. A running bath.

Any regrets?

That we are as similar in death as life, clustered here under the same headstones. But, to tell the truth, I never wanted to stand out. I would hate to have seen those newspaper reports with my name in them and the neighbours no doubt saying how quiet I was and the bishop praying for my soul and the police confirming I had no subversive connections.

Anything else you miss?

The smell of life given off by the earth that I have no nose for here. Those moments of nylon softness at bedtime nothing had prepared me to expect. The sports results.

Finally, do you forgive your killer?

I accept death as I accepted life - as something to get on with.

CHARLIE DONNELLY

Charles Patrick Donnelly was born in Co Tyrone in July 1914. He was killed on February 27, 1937, at the Jarama Front while fighting for the Spanish Republic. In 1987 Charlie's brother, Joseph, prepared a book, "Charlie Donnelly: The Life & Poems", which was published by The Dedalus Press. .

"We ran for cover ... Charlie Donnelly of the Irish Company is crouched behind an olive tree. He has picked up a bunch of olives from the ground and is squeezing them. I hear him say something quietly during a lull in machine-gun fire: Even the olives are bleeding."

That sentence spoken by Donnelly moments before he died has become one of the best-known phrases of that terrible conflict in Spain. Charlie Donnelly had been an arts student in University College, Dublin where, among his contemporaries, Denis Devlin and Brian Coffey were students. By then Donnelly was making speeches condemning the rise of Fascism in Europe, and he was an active member of the Republican Congress. He also met, and fell in love with, Cora Hughes whose father was a close friend of DeValera. In July 1934 Donnelly was imprisoned for two weeks on charges arising from a picket on a factory where the workers were striking for the right to form a union. Again in 1935 he was given a prison sentence for a similar offence. Later that year he left Dublin for London and late in December began to make his way to Spain.

In his short life Charlie Donnelly achieved an intensity of action and thought denied to most other people. His poems are few but they are intense and carefully wrought. His last poems showed a power of thought and feeling and a control of his medium that promised a fine development had he lived.

TO YOU

In the old days of bitter faces
And cold eyes,
I would go to the lone, large places, the hills
And the skies,
To the twilights of grey, great shadows
And bird cries ...
And shadows would hide me, and the wind sighed
With my sighs ...
But you, my Jewess, having come, and gone,
Whence can I bring my soul,
When the winds but mock, and the shadows
Bring mirrors of thy soul?

AT THE DREAMING OF THE DREAMS

My dreams are dreaming, and the sacred books
Have closed their lips, and smothered up their lies,
And all the worlds are whirling in the skies,
And all the skies are like a woman's looks.

I live, I live, and yet I reck it not
I am one with the depths and with the heights,
I am beyond the fadings of the lights
Of all the suns. I live, and yet live not.

The murmur of the waters of all Being
Is me; the silence of undying Death.
Eternity breathes in me, and its breath
Is Death in hand with Life, Unbeing with Being.

The bosom of God's parent, boundless Sleep,
Enfolds me, and I drown within the eyes,
The smiling eyes that are a woman's eyes,
The eyes of all the soul of all the Deep.

And all the dreamings of the dreams of God
Are burning from me, like a woman's love,
I fade and melt in Space, below, above,
And God is in my being, I in God.

Oh, all men's toil to prove true the great lie
Of the world, like staring in a sea
To find the secret of its blue, while He
Above, reflects it from the waters of His eye.

Oh, all the world is but an endless lie,
Eternity and Space a swirling dream.
My soul is like the murmur of a stream
I dream within a dream. To live, to die,
To be, or not to be, matters not, dream I.

IN A LIBRARY

Are the moods voiceless? For I have no words.
Blood cannot talk, although it crack the skin.
Red hots and colds are pumped up from the pit
Like hungering men; and no word-woman being near,
    sink again howling in.
And I fume, and look outside on the grey
Wind hammered to fantasy day.

WAGES OF DEVIATION

Diffident labour of poetry,
perilous pleasure of the tightened mind,
youth's lonely, austere joy
were broken by your hands
bringing elation, opening
through the white summer roads, the world.

Through love's complications we,
intricacy of touch and speech —
when touch acquired the delicacy of speech
and speech invaded apprehending flesh —
wove, wove together.

Life as a game between us,
through uninterrupted years,
we dreamed
under the twilit trees, when broke
the questing labour of desire,
in intimacy on the blood.

Now there's resentment, purpose crossed,
heart's outcry of tears in the street,
contracted heart distorts the world.
Or truce declared, your memory,
hair blown fine against lamplight, makes
my heart and hands go wild.

THE TOLERANCE OF CROWS

Death comes in quantity from solved
Problems on maps, well-ordered dispositions,
Angles of elevation and direction;

Comes innocent from tools children might
Love, retaining under pillows,
Innocently impales on any flesh.

And with flesh falls apart the mind
That trails thought from the mind that cuts
Thought clearly for a waiting purpose.

Progress of poison in the nerves and
Discipline's collapse is halted.
Body awaits the tolerance of crows.

POEM

Between rebellion as a private study and the public
Defiance, is simple action only on which will flickers
Catlike, for spring. Whether at nerve-roots is secret
Iron, there's no diviner can tell, only the moment can show.
Simple and unclear moment, on a morning utterly different
And under circumstances different from what you'd expected.

Your flag is public over granite. Gulls fly above it.
Whatever the issue of the battle is, your memory
Is public, for them to pull awry with crooked hands,
Moist eyes. And village reputations will be built on
Inaccurate accounts of your campaign. You're name for orators,
Figure stone-struck beneath damp Dublin sky.

In a delaying action, perhaps, on hillside in remote parish,
Outposts correctly placed, retreat secured to wood, bridge mined
Against pursuit, sniper may sight you carelessly contoured.
Or death may follow years in strait confinement, where diet
Is uniform as ceremony, lacking only fruit.
Or on the barrack square before the sun casts shadow.

Name, subject of all-considered words, praise and blame
Irrelevant, the public talk which sounds the same on hollow
Tongue as true, you'll be with Parnell and with Pearse.
Name aldermen will raise a cheer with, teachers make reference
Oblique in class, and boys and women spin gum of sentiment
On qualities attributed in error.

Man, dweller in mountain huts, possessor of coloured mice,
Skilful in minor manual turns, patron of obscure subjects, of
Gaelic swordsmanship and mediaeval armoury.
The technique of the public man, the masked servilities are
Not for you. Master of military trade, you give
Like Raleigh, Lawrence, Childers, your services but not yourself.

HEROIC HEART

Ice of heroic heart seals plasmic soil
Where things ludicrously take root
To show in leaf kindness time had buried
And cry music under a storm of 'planes,
Making thrust head to slacken, muscle waver
And intent mouth recall old tender tricks.
Ice of heroic heart seals steel-bound brain.

There newer organs built for friendship's grappling
Waste down like wax. There only leafless plants
And earth retain disinterestedness.
Thought, magnetised to lie of the land, moves
Heartily over the map wrapped in its iron
Storm. Battering the roads, armoured columns
Break walls of stone or bone without receipt.
Jawbones find new ways with meat, loins
Raking and blind, new ways with women.

PATRICK O'BRIEN

Patrick O'Brien was born in Claremorris, Co. Mayo. He was educated locally and at St. Jarlath's College, Tuam. He is a priest in the Archdiocese of Tuam. He has served on Clare Island and is working currently in Skehana, East Galway. In 1984 he published "Diary of a Central American Visit". In 1988 The Dedalus Press published his first collection, "A Book of Genesis". He is currently editing a selection of poems by Father Daniel Berrigan to be published by The Dedalus Press in 1992.

DIPTYCH

1. Sputnik (for Martin)

We returned, to find the birthday cake
baked to perfection, the kitchen air rich
with diced fruit and good enough to bite.
And our youngest brother missing. We take
a room each, cupboards, corners, every niche
revealing an absence and a growing fright.

We found him outside the house, in a back
garden. On the black, pecked ground beside
him an emptied bottle of brandy;
hens and chickens reeling in a maniac
dance, Martin, aged five, their stupefied
choreographer, humming "Yankee Doodle Dandy".

That night, brother uneasily asleep,
we stood in that same spot staring into the sky.
Our eyes, the world, dilating in the dark
and moving slowly across the deep
dream of space. My parents' words were lullaby
for their age where time was marked

In days and hours and months and years
and light came straight over the half-doors.
Moving stars meant only infinities
of grace and redemption of their tears.
I began to run, orbiting their disorder.
My mind weightless, drunk with possibilities.

2. Cuba (for John)

Half-past five, closing-time, the factory
goes quiet. The last pig has screamed
into the brutal air. Bristles mat
the cooling waters of a tank. The crematory

furnace expires. The day's kill is streamed
into refrigerated rooms, to await
the long knives of morning. Bicycles
whisper on the gravel as workers
leave. I loved that hour, the freedom
in their faces, hard yet open, the oracles
of blood they spoke that made me wonder.
They tossed me half-crowns of coin and wisdom.

One evening they passed without a word
or gift, lips tight on some secret
too terrible to tell. One stopped and said
"Go home to your parents, have you not heard
the world ends tonight". Eyes had the regret
of graveyard mornings for all that is dead

or about to die. At home the talk
was of Kennedy, Cuba, missiles.
We were learning the dialect of despair —
strange words, long sobbing silences, a walk
in the night air knowing exile
from our future. Time closing in a grip of fear.

RIGHT OF REPLY, WOMEN OF JERUSALEM

O, let us grieve for what is griefstricken.
Do not imagine that tears come easy.
We are hardened by city and its men's
impetuous dreams. Each day new frenzies
grip them. Is it from fear of home
they run after every new prophet?
And fear of what future brings down their doom
on every dream? They will soon forget

you, and our tears will memorise your brief
ascendency. We are mothers in deep
mourning for all that is weak and fragile.
Something in you spoke a common exile.
It is our children that we see and weep
for in your face. All are one in our grief.

CHILDREN'S GAME, GUATAJIAGUA, EL SALVADOR

(to Skehana Macra)

Heat has kilned the red earth
to the rough texture of pottery;
the rain season glazed on the surface
footprints of child and man, the lottery

of war, soldier and guerrilla in turn
imprinting their design. Whose slogan
was last half erased? What flag burns
over the civic building? When children

begin to play such questions cease.
In their faces battles and conquests
long ago have made a treaty of peace,
Spain and Pipil Indian at rest

in the delicate structures of bone.
They make a small circle in the ground.
Then three strides out a larger one.
Dead centre they place small coins.

There are three of them, each with a spinning-
top, hand-carved in hard wood
from forests which heard first the new tongue
and first knew the iron name of the iron God.

All is circular, coins and tops, the games
bounds. And overhead the sun keeps
vigilant eye on lands which once flamed
to its glory. Sun sweat and weeping

moon were gold and silver filigree —
not to be sold or bartered
but to be the labour and love of beauty.
The coins are the history of what happened.

The top is spun, orbiting planet, star-
fall, quick, sure. A dime flies outward
for the Aztec warrior. Childs laughter,
and the piazza is innocent of war.

We gather to marvel at the skill,
a cupped palm enfolds the still
spinning top and the game continues
until the last coin is spun from the circle.

Sun and fun are suddenly eclipsed,
an ill wind blows and a giant insect
shadow prowls. In the shattered sky
the spinning top of helicopters are cyclops eyes

with children in their deadly aim and sight.

ON THAT DAY

On that day of freedom and equality
avoid the streets of the city,
loud with celebrations.

Go, rather, to the sea's shore,
as you did on all the days before,
and hear its quiet cautions.

WOUNDED ANGELS

(after a painting by Cecil Collins)
to Noel Dermot O'Donoghue

There must be houses
where wounded angels rest,
half-way places where drowsing
spirits are the only guests;

They will be on the edge
of landscapes, say, at cliff-fall
where the bravest voyage
crashed, or, where snows wall

up against the universe.
Let them lay their wings
where lately cindered cities converse
with their dead and the dead sing

with angel voices of the earth
a deserted village in the Burren
with alpine plants in cold hearths;
jungle temples where gods turn

in the slow anonymity of time
and men have left for known
or unknown reasons. Poor shrines
on desperate roads, habitations thrown

like wild dice against the odds
of space and time. Such places,
and others where pathos gnawed
the heart and tears furrowed faces

to the naked bone of a truth —
between flesh and its word there
are transsubstantiations, mute
and broken-winged and bare.

There must be houses
where wounded Angels rest.
Or how else may we rejoice
on a planet cold and unblessed?

EVER AFTER

I will tell you how it ends.
I am the man who was the child
who spoke aloud the emperor's nakedness.
I have lived to regret the words. Friends
became distant, disappeared. My name was filed
away for future reference. A great sadness

began in our land. A twenty year terror.
The laughter of the crowd at my remark
quickly turned to tears — martial law
applied with ferocity. It is said the emperor
took personal responsibility for the dark
age. Executions and reprisals he oversaw,

with eyes turned cruel. The day I came of age
his soldiers brought an invitation to the palace.
They threw me into prison, stripped my clothes.
Each night he visits me in my cold cage.
His splendid uniforms are bemedalled. What solace
is mine when, nightly, the doors close.

HAD I BUT KNOWN

(from the Russian of Boris Pasternak)

Had I but known in the early morning
of my youth that poetry is written
in blood, and its lines are in mourning
for all that is good but forbidden

I would never have put pen to paper.
But then it seemed no more than a game
to amuse the child-like maker
and, with luck, bring a measure of fame.

But in the coliseum of life and death
the empires give thumbs down to poetry
demanding only its last poor breath
in the circus rings of revelry.

However, passion is master of my lines
and onto its boards I will tread
there where life and art I will define
in words that earth and fate have said.

PADRAIG J.DALY

Born in Dungarvan, Co Waterford, in 1943, he is now working as an Augustinian priest in Dublin. He has published several collections of poetry, including "Poems: Selected and New", The Dedalus Press 1988. A selection of his poems was translated into Italian by Margherita Guidacci and published in Rome.

We have, I believe, as humans, a need to praise, a need to celebrate the miracle of the world around us. Without praise and celebration, we frustrate something deep within ourselves. Creation is wide and various. In us it becomes conscious of itself. We give it tongue. Thomas Merton once remarked that he was "in a condition of ecstasy over the human race". That ecstasy over humanity, over the world, is for me the first impulse of poetry.

But the world is also a baffling place. Every answer leads to fresh questioning. Today's secure truths carry the postulates of tomorrow's conundrums. But where logic fails, poetry (drawing on heart and gut as well as head) helps us find meanings.

Poetry communicates states of feeling, states of being, states of interaction with one another and with the world. It puts a name on loss, loneliness, pleasure, pain. Through it we communicate the truth of ourselves.

I am convinced that much anguish is caused in today's world by our having lost touch with our creativity. In mental hospitals people are put making handbags and pots in an attempt to restore them to themselves and to help them transcend themselves. Poetry can serve a similar purpose.

Matisse, an agnostic, was challenged once for accepting a religious commission. "When I paint," he replied, "I work in a state analogous to prayer". For me, poetry is prayer — my way of expressing the truth of myself, of celebrating creation and Creator, of coming to terms with the world's mystery and pain.

-Padraig J. Daly

PROBLEM

I understand Francis — all the stuff about the birds,
Throwing his clothes at his father; the singing, praising heart.

Once I travelled from Rome into Umbria
To his towns, his green mountains,
His fast streams,

Saw the coarse cloth he wore against cold,
The chapel shrining Chiara's hair.

Teresa Sanchez was never a problem:
In convent or covered wagon
In constant seesaw up and down towards God.

Or John
Soaring through his bars like a linnet in song.

But I am blind still to the Jew
My life traipses after;
And the spacelessness of God
Hesitates the hand I reach
Behind cross and tabernacle

Into his paltry loneliness.

EVENING AT OSTIA

(*In memory of Pier Paolo Pasolini*)

When evening came, the red flowers were watered
on the balconies; the air was heavy with their scent.
The overflow dripped softly to the pavings, like rainfall.
People came out now to walk in the coolness.

Tablecloths were spread outside the trattorie;
Under a stark white bulb, a man sold triangles of melon;
Microphones blared songs of tenderness from a circus tent:
Lions jumped, seals went through hoops, horses galloped
    on the sawdust.

The wineshops were open well into dark.
You could still smell the long flitches
Of the morning's bread. Someone argued far above;
Through a window, a new Caruso was singing.

There were notices forbidding people onto the pier.
Fishermen and lovers climbed, laughing,
Past the barriers; the sea itself
Was feverish and warm.

Cars sped by with their midnight revellers,
Brakes screeched at every crossing;
The crowds had gathered to where the light was,
The deckchairs were all folded, the sand raked clean.

So if he cried out, from this his last wilderness,
There was no one to hear.

MAGNIFICAT FOR CATHERINE

Your mother's body
Softly glowing as alabaster,
You danced in her eyes.

Before ever you saw light
Or learned to scream
So lustily,

When you were totally unwashed,
I watched you
Move beneath her body.

Swimming in primeval fluid,
Sole inhabitant
Of your close and shadowy universe;

And when I reached out my hand
To touch you,
You kicked at me suddenly

Till like those mountain women
In our book,
I heard my words becoming song.

JOURNEY

Day after day
The caravans move through the hot sun
To the clay-walled city:

The walls rise suddenly where the desert ends,
Sharp shapes cut out of sun and shadow:

Animal after animal,
Huge relentless camels,
The children in light dresses running to keep pace.

These people have crossed treacherous passes and have lived;
They have followed rockstrewn roads
By steep cliff-faces.

They have lost animals to rain and thunderstorm
When the hard mountain floated like a torrent under them.

Here and there where grass is lushest
They make camp,
Sit at fires by night singing,
Prepare bread for their journey.

But always they must move;
And still they move:

If a man grows old among them
And the paths are steep and the ways impassable,
He will sit in some barren place
And sing himself calmly into death.

But always the caravans go onward;
Here at the gate there is laughter,
The women chatter,
There will be trading for flour and cloth;

They will salute old friends,
Exchange beads and trinkets;
A marriage will be celebrated into the long starry night-time.

But at the end, at every end,
They must go onward
As if ahead somewhere were destination;

And somewhere stillness.

ENCOUNTER

Monotony of sun
On sand and scrub,
A place of wild beasts
And long shadows:

At last he comes
To green and olivegroves,
Vineyards,
Houses climbing beyond walls
Along a hillside.

Here the tempter waits,
Full of candour,
Offering for easy sale
All the green kingdoms of the world.

And he,
Though gaunt from fasting,
Needing rest,

Some perfect star
Seen a lifetime back
Determining him,

Passes slowly by.

AMONG THE NETTLES

When we turn our backs to the sea,
It trembles still and climbs and falters;

On quiet hillsides families of foxes
Sport at evening
Where green pines slice the sun.

Glorious butterflies flit where no one watches,
Dun horses ramble by rivers and shake miraculous manes.

The willow grouse sits on her eggs all day
And holds her breath when danger comes
And stills at her will the beating of her heart.

In lakes far into the marshland
The glebe treads water in his courtship dance.

All day long the world is tumbling,
Stars follow their ordered ways,
Clouds form and reform.

A mind moves endlessly among the nettles
Full of the thrive of leaf and flower,

Hardly breathing or heaving,
Still as the willowgrouse.

GUARD

Once you go under the arch,
It is as if you were never elsewhere;
And the world of sparkling lawns,
Children cracking open eggs,
Squabbling through the half-sleep of breakfast-time,
Never existed.

You take on sin with your uniform;
And you float away from love
Like a legendary swimmer caught in currents
That drag him to a dismal underworld
Where life is lived in caverns
And bats spring eerily out of shadows.

And if you try to reach out,
Something constrains your stretching arms;
And you have no voice for voicing tenderness.

The greatest danger comes
When you carry your underworld back out;
And the brightness of grass
And flowers and eggs
And your own children laughing
No longer touches you.

JUNE 1943: PAUSE AT ÖTZAL

We were in a valley between two peaks;
Snow glittered on the high wastes.

In the fields women were piking hay onto poles,
Trees were giant keepers of stillness.

Gentle Austrian voices spoke along the platform,
Another train shunted near,
People crossed to our empty carriages.

Soughing softly we moved again:
An old man near me murmured a psalm.

Never before was murder so innocently done.

REMEMBERING MY FATHER

1.
When they thinned the woods,
Dormant bluebells sprang up everywhere;

This Summer, four perfect lilies
Came suddenly in the garden
Where no one had planted them;

In the grass beneath my window,
Some small invisible thing beats insistent wings:

Your silence is full of signals.

2.

Going to see you in Cork was the worst,
Your memory gone, your light faded.

The ward was in the dungeon of the hospital,
The chairs fitting tightly by the beds
So everyone could hear when we talked.

The doctors were always absent;
The nurses humoured you like an imbecile child.

How could I explain to them
That you shone like the Daystar once?:
We basked like fat fishes in your brilliance.

3.

No matter how much you walked at the end,
Your lungs were thwarted by the flowering cancers.

When I recalled tales from your past,
You begged me to write them down

So you could hold them like rails to lift yourself again.

4.

Four weeks before you died,
You wanted to see the graves in Ring.

I had forgotten where they were;
But you, whose memory was gone for recent things,
Walked me to them across the uneven ground.

Later, near Kenneally's,
You spoke "Na Prátaí Dubha" word for word.

I wept as you recalled the breaking up of a world;
But for a closer breaking.

5.
We can see Leagh from the churchyard
And the gaudy cornfields of Gortnadiha.

The tide is full in the Bay,
Boats sail by the Cunnigar.

You could never comprehend our need to be elsewhere
With all this blossoming world about us.

Geese sit on the sea,
Dunlins move in gusts along the shore,
Water laps against stone:

Your silence is full of signals.

PENTIMENTO

1.
He created emptiness first;
Then threw the world out like wool
To dangle amid the planets.

From the wet earth,
He drew animals, bats,
Fish and coloured birds.

To one only,
He gave a mind to range the stars;
But bound by clay and death and foolishness.

Sitting back, he laughed;
While men and women
Built draughty palaces.

2.
Beyond the far reaches of the heavens
He is gone;

Beyond the last planet and star,
Where everything is wind and dust.

We cry out;
But if he hears,
He moves away from our voices.

3.
He returns once more from the hunt,
With dead wildfowl braced across his shoulders,
Whistling as he goes.

A lone grayhound precedes him,
Scenting us out,
Warning him of our approach.

VALENTIN IREMONGER

Valentin Iremonger was born in Sandymount on 14 February, 1918, not a stone's throw from where W.B.Yeats was born. He worked most of his working life in the Department of Foreign Affairs, Dublin, ending up as Ambassador to Sweden (and concurrently to Norway and Finland 1964-73), to Luxembourg (1973-79) and to Portugal. He retired in 1980 and lived in Dublin. He died in 1991

Valentin Iremonger won the AE Memorial Award in 1945 for a collection later published by Envoy Magazine, Dublin, MacMillan, London and the St Martin's Press in New York. Reviews included an essay length review by Raymond Mortimer in The Sunday Times: "All I can do is to touch on some characteristics in the works of Mr Iremonger who seems to me a writer with gifts much above the average ..."

In 1972 The Dolmen Press published "Horan's Field and Other Reservations". Iremonger's work has been represented in anthologies on both sides of the Atlantic. He edited, with Robert Greacen, "Contemporary Irish Poetry", Faber and Faber 1949 and also "Irish Short Stories", Faber 1960.

In 1988 The Dedalus Press published "Sandymount, Dublin", a gathering of the poems that Iremonger would like to see preserved as representing the best of his work. His poems have strongly influenced later generations of poets and he was held in great esteem both as person and poet.

THIS HOURE HER VIGILL

Elizabeth, frigidly stretched,
On a spring day surprised us
With her starched dignity and the quietness
Of her hands clasping a black cross.

With book and candle and holy water dish
She received us in the room with the blind down.
Her eyes were peculiarly closed and we knelt shyly
Noticing the blot of her hair on the white pillow.

We met that evening by the crumbling wall
In the field behind the house where I lived
And talked it over, but could find no reason
Why she had left us whom she had liked so much.

Death, yes, we understood: something to do
With age and decay, decrepit bodies;
But here was this vigorous one, aloof and prim,
Who would not answer our furtive whispers.

Next morning, hearing the priest call her name,
I fled outside, being full of certainty,
And cried my seven years against the church's stone wall.
For eighteen years I did not speak her name

Until this autumn day when, in a gale,
A sapling fell outside my window, its branches
Rebelliously blotting the lawn's green. Suddenly, I thought
Of Elizabeth, frigidly stretched.

ON SANDYMOUNT STRAND

These long years
Watching the seagulls bank and retreat daily
And the tide's remorseless flowing on the wrinkled
Forehead of the strand, I have been happy here,
Stealing apples from orchards and being chased,
Playing football and more mysterious games
Lost to me now, or breaking my heart
For a girl who broke her eight-year life she was so eager
To live and to experience everything well.

And there was poetry. When I found
Lines detonating in my mind and my pen
Stabbing the pages of my memory, I would have sold
My sister to the devil for a poem
Complete and lucid as spring-water, to startle
God and rock his golden throne.
It never came; yet I was happy, too,
With the snapping swords of words and the shields
    of tinsel phrases.

Gone, now, the adolescent swagger and closed
The book of my youth, ruled, and a trial
Balance extracted for my future use.
I thought to-day
As still the gulls banked and the evil tide
Crept nearer from the horizon while I walked
By Sandymount Tower, now decrepit and strewn
With rubble borne there by the wind and water,
How my youth wore down like an old shoe-sole
Sodden with age,
Leaving between me and the hostile, hard
Ground of society, nothing — nothing at all
Now to prevent the damp and the needling chill
Eating into my bones and burrowing to my heart.

THE GULL

Some bitch of a bird yelled dog's abuse
At me this morning when I woke up.
Flat on my back I listened, stunned
By the bad-tempered tirade that never stopped

Once even for breath or to choose a word.
From her tongue's tip a sailor's range
Of invective, blue as the sky, spearing towards me
Slewed and ricochetted against the window pane,

As she made her own of the five-tone scale
With a design of grace-notes no coal-quay shawlie
Could shuffle together on a sunny morning
Or drunk in a pub in an evening's brawling.

This was what I had feared all along;
Trick-o-the-loop Nature, street-angel, house-devil.
Well I guessed the sheen on the far green hills
To be the smooth evil of satin, its moral level.

So while, at the window, a wicked bird frantically
Crumpled the morning tissue of silence, I resolved
To put as much distance between Nature's red claws
And myself as the years could make possible.

For me the Queensberry game, the built-up manner, the artificial,
Will be some vantage-point from which to view the wild,
Afford delaying actions while I make some judgements
Uninfluenced by the terror of a child,

And, in due course, questioned, I'll reply
That the great white bird with the cruel beak was to blame
Who, one sunny quiet morning in May, suddenly frightened me,
Roaring, cursing and spitting against the window-pane.

HECTOR

Talking to her, he knew it was the end,
The last time he'd speed her into sleep with kisses:
Achilles had it in for him and was fighting mad.
The roads of his longing she again wandered,
A girl desirable as midsummer's day.

He was a marked man and he knew it,
Being no match for Achilles whom the gods were backing.
Sadly he spoke to her for hours, his heart
Snapping like sticks, she on his shoulder crying.
Yet, sorry only that the meaning eluded him,

He slept well all night, having caressed
Andromache like a flower, though in a dream he saw
A body lying on the sands, huddled and bleeding,
Near the feet a sword in bits and by the head
An upturned, dented helmet.

ICARUS

As, even today, the airman, feeling the plane sweat
Suddenly, seeing the horizon tilt up gravely, the wings shiver,
Knows that, for once, Daedalus has slipped up badly
Drunk on the job, perhaps, more likely dreaming,
    high-flier Icarus,
Head butting down, skidding along the light-shafts
Back, over the tones of the sea-waves and the slip-stream, heard
The gravel-voiced, stuttering trumpets of his heart

Sennet among the crumbling court-yards of his brain the mistake
Of trusting somebody else on an important affair like this;
And, while the flat sea, approaching, buckled into oh! avenues
Of acclamation, he saw the wrong story fan out into history,
Truth, undefined, lost in his own neglect. On the hills,
The summer-shackled hills, the sun spanged all day;
Love and the world were young and there was no ending:

But star-chaser, big-time-going, chancer Icarus
Like a dog on the sea lay and the girls forgot him,

And Daedalus, too busy hammering another job,
Remembered him only in pubs. No bugler at all
Sobbed taps for the young fool then, reported missing,
Presumed drowned, wing-bones and feathers on the tide
Drifting in casually, one by one.

TIME, THE FAITHLESS

All evening, while the summer trees were crying
Their sudden realisation of the spring's sad death,
Somewhere a clock was ticking and we heard it here
In the sun-porch, where we sat so long, buying
Thoughts for a penny from each other. Near
Enough it was and loud to make us talk beneath our breath.

And a time for quiet talking it was, to be sure, although
The rain would have drowned the sound of our combined
      voices.
The spring of our youth that night suddenly died
And summer filled the veins of our lives like slow
Water into creeks edging. Like the trees you cried.
Autumn and winter, you said, had so many disguises

And how could we be always on the watch to plot
A true perspective for each minute's value? I couldn't reply,
So many of my days toppled into the past, unnoticed.
Silence like sorrow multiplied around you, a lot
Of whose days counted so much. My heart revolted
That time for you should be such a treacherous ally

And though, midnight inclining bells over the city
With a shower of sound like tambourines of Spain
Gay in the teeth of the night air, I thought
Of a man who said the truth was in the pity,
Somehow, under the night's punched curtain, I was lost.
I only knew the pity and the pain.

DENIS DEVLIN

Denis Devlin was born in Scotland in 1908 and in 1920 the family returned to Ireland. In 1926 he entered the diocesan seminary, All Hallow's College, in Dublin, leaving again in 1927. He studied at UCD and was awarded an MA in 1931. In 1930 he published *Poems*, with Brian Coffey. He studied at the Sorbonne and worked for a time in UCD. In 1935 he entered the Department of Foreign Affairs; in 1938 he was posted to Rome as first secretary. In 1939 he was made consul in New York. He worked as minister plenipotentiary in Italy and in Turkey and in 1958 was named ambassador to Italy. He died from leukaemia in Dublin in 1959. In 1989 The Dedalus Press published "Collected Poems of Denis Devlin", edited by J.C.C.Mays.

—"In Ireland, the thirties were dominated on the one hand by W.B.Yeats and such later Twilighters as Oliver St. John Gogarty and F.R.Higgins, and on the other by young writers — Austin Clarke and Patrick Kavanagh, among the poets — who were intent on modifying the agenda set by their elders. Those who differently looked to Joyce as an exemplary figure, and who were not content to work Joyce's early realisitc vein, found little support. They mostly went abroad, and their recognition at home was delayed to the nineteen-sixties. I refer, of course, to Samuel Beckett, Denis Devlin and Brian Coffey...

.....Devlin was self-consciously and proudly an Irish poet, though self-consciousness and pride are checked by self-possession and restraint. Again, his reputation as a difficult and particularly literary poet has obscured the fact that the way he wrote makes sophisticated political commentary, if that is what readers are looking for....

.....Devlin stands for a kind of poetry which sets the surrounding, better-known tradition in perspective. It is dedicated to art before self-interest or self-expression. It is moved by contained confidence that does not have to seek for reassurance or curry favour. It contains values which might be said to be Irish, though they are unlikely to appeal to tour-operators or politicians.....

.....For Devlin, even to think in terms of a national literary tradition is provincial and limiting. His aim was like that of Joyce in fiction, to take the world as his province. Devlin looked to the writers from whom he took his bearings in the same way as Joyce looked to Hauptmann and Ibsen, Flaubert and Vico. They are writers against whom a writer measures his position — not from whom he borrows or hides behind. The result is, in Devlin's as in Joyce's case, a kind of writing which is less against its time than outside it. It is not a programmatic deviation from other writing of the nineteen-thirties but instead proceeds on a different, classic premise." —

from the introduction, by J.C.C.Mays, to "Collected Poems of Denis Devlin".

LOUGH DERG

The poor in spirit on their rosary rounds,
The jobbers with their whiskey-angered eyes,
The pink bank clerks, the tip-hat papal counts,
And drab, kind women their tonsured mockery tries,
Glad invalids on penitential feet
Walk the Lord's majesty like their village street.

With mullioned Europe shattered, this Northwest,
Rude-sainted isle would pray it whole again:
(Peasant Apollo! Troy is worn to rest.)
Europe that humanized the sacred bane
Of God's chance who yet laughed in his mind
And balanced thief and saint: were they this kind?

Low rocks, a few weasels, lake
Like a field of burnt gorse; the rooks caw;
Ours, passive, for man's gradual wisdom take
Firefly instinct dreamed out into law;
The prophets' jewelled kingdom down at heel
Fires no Augustine here. Inert, they kneel;

All is simple and symbol in their world,
The incomprehended rendered fabulous.
Sin teases life whose natural fruits withheld
Sour the deprived nor bloom for timely loss:
Clan Jansen! less what magnanimity leavens
Man's wept-out, fitful, magniloquent heavens

Where prayer was praise, O Lord! the Temple trumpets
Cascaded down Thy sunny pavilions of air,
The scroll-tongued priests, the galvanic strumpets,
All clash and stridency gloomed upon Thy stair;
The pharisees, the exalted boy their power
Sensually psalmed in Thee, their coming hour!

And to the sun, earth turned her flower of sex,
Acanthus in the architects' limpid angles;
Close priests allegorized the Orphic egg's
Brood, and from the Academy, tolerant wranglers
Could hear the contemplatives of the Tragic Choir
Drain off man's sanguine, pastoral death-desire.

It was said stone dreams and animal sleeps and man
Is awake; but sleep with its drama on us bred
Animal articulate, only somnambulist can
Conscience like Cawdor give the blood its head
For the dim moors to reign through druids again.
O first geometer! tangent-feelered brain

Clearing by inches the encircled eyes,
Bolder than the peasant tiger whose autumn beauty
Sags in the expletive kill, or the sacrifice
Of dearth puffed positive in the stance of duty
With which these pilgrims would propitiate
Their fears; no leafy, medieval state

Of paschal cathedrals backed on earthy hooves
Against the craftsmen's primary-coloured skies
Whose gold was Gabriel on the patient roofs,
The parabled windows taught the dead to rise,
And Christ the Centaur, in two natures whole,
With fable and proverb joinered body and soul.

Water withers from the oars. The pilgrims blacken
Out of the boats to masticate their sin
Where Dante smelled among the stones and bracken
The door to Hell (O harder Hell where pain
Is earthed, a casuist sanctuary of guilt!).
Spirit bureaucracy on a bet built

Part by this race when monks in convents of coracles
For the Merovingian centuries left their land,
Belled, fragrant; and honest in their oracles
Bespoke the grace to give without demand,
Martyrs Heaven winged nor tempted with reward.
And not ours, doughed in dogma, who never have dared

Will with surrogate palm distribute hope:
No better nor worse than I who, in my books,
Have angered at the stake with Bruno and, by the rope
Watt Tyler swung from, leagued with shifty looks
To fuse the next rebellion with the desperate
Serfs in the sane need to eat and get;

Have praised, on its thunderous canvas, the Florentine smile
As man took to wearing his death, his own,
Sapped crisis through cathedral branches (while
Flesh groped loud round dissenting skeleton)
In soul, reborn as body's appetite:
Now languish back in body's amber light,

Now is consumed. O earthly paradise!
Hell is to know our natural empire used
Wrong, by mind's moulting, brute divinities.
The vanishing tiger's saved, his blood transfused.
Kent is for Jutes again and Glasgow town
Burns high enough to screen the stars and moon.

Well may they cry who have been robbed, their wasting
Shares in justice legally lowered until
Man his own actor, matrix, mould and casting,
Or man, God's image, sees his idol spill.
Say it was pride that did it, or virtue's brief:
To them that suffer it is no relief.

All indiscriminate, man, stone, animal
Are woken up in nightmare. What John the Blind
From Patmos saw works and we speak it. Not all
The men of God nor the priests of mankind
Can mend or explain the good and broke, not one
Generous with love prove communion;

Behind the eyes the winged ascension flags,
For want of spirit by the market blurbed,
And if hands touch, such fraternity sags
Frightened this side the dykes of death disturbed
Like Aran Islands' bibulous, unclean seas:
Pietà: but the limbs ache; it is not peace.

Then to see less, look little, let hearts' hunger
Feed on water and berries. The pilgrims sing:
Life will fare well from elder to younger,
Though courage fail in a world-end, rosary ring.
Courage kills its practitioners and we live,
Nothing forgotten, nothing to forgive,

We pray to ourself. The metal moon, unspent
Virgin eternity sleeping in the mind,
Excites the form of prayer without content;
Whitethorn lightens, delicate and blind,
The negro mountain, and so, knelt on her sod,
This woman beside me murmuring *My God! My God!*

ENCOUNTER

"Our saints are poets, Milton and Blake,
Who would rib men with pride against the spite
Of God," the Englishman said, and in the silence
Hatred sparkled along our bones. He said:
"Celt, your saints adorn the poor with roses
And praise God for standing still."

Between the two of us, François from Touraine,
Where women and the wheat ripen and fall due
Suavely at evening, smiled, teasing the breadcrumbs.
He whispered: "Patience; listen to the world's
Growth, resulting in fire and childlike water!"

And I: "Milton and Marvell, like the toady, Horace,
Praised the men of power for the good
They happened on, with bible and sword; the wretched
Hold out their begging-bowls at the wooden gates,
Too poor to weep, too poor to weep with tears."

Boxflower scent. Fumes of burgundy.
Nagging children at the tables
A dream's remove from their fathers smoking
Along the boulevard laid with yellow evening.

FROM GOVERNMENT BUILDINGS

Evening lapses. No pity or pain, the badgered
Great get home, and the little, tomorrow's anchorage,
All smiling, sour the milk of charity,
Like the pyrrhonist poets, Love's saboteurs.

The clerks fan out and the lamps; and I look inwards:
What turns amuse you now? with whom, not me! do
You cower in Time, whose palsied pulse is nimbler
A hair's breadth when want and have are equal?

My room sighs empty with malignant waiting;
The November wind slows down outside, wheeling
Twig and awning on the brick balcony,
A wind with hackles up. In Rome at evening

Swallows traced eggshapes on the vellum sky,
The wind was warm with blue rain in Dublin;
When the culture-heroes explored the nether world
It was voiceless beasts on the move made Death terrible.

Friendship I will not, barring you; to have witness does:
Doll birds, dogs with their social nose, by day
Are touchstone. But at night my totem silence
With face of wood refuses to testify.

The famous exile's dead, from many on many
Deportations, from Spain to Prague to Nice,
Kaleidoscopic police, his Danse Macabre;
One of the best the worst had never feared.

You, you I cherish with my learned heart
As in the bombed cathedral town, doubly
A tourist trophy now, the dean shouted: "At last!
At least and at last we have stored the windows away,

The fabulation of my Lord's glory, by
Seven and by seven and by seven multiplied!"
So is my care though none your mystic I,
Nor you like the painted saints but breath and more.

And do not pace the room haunting the future
But be my insular love; and I would have you
Fingering the ring with its silver bat, the foreign
And credible Chinese symbol of happiness.

from THE HEAVENLY FOREIGNER

NOTRE DAME DE PARIS

There is nothing now that will buy Him off;
The singers of life who are the memory of life
Are silenced by the scream of plant, tree, sea;
The beautiful severed head floats downriver;
The land recedes
With all its needy industry of wheat and vine;
With her weaving spells out of the spell of her speech,
Weaving charm out of the charm of her body;
The day recedes with all my adorations.

How she stood, hypothetical-eyed and metaphor-breasted,
Weaving my vision out of my sight,
Out of my sight, out of my very sight,
Out of her sight,
Till the sight I see with is blind with light
Other than hers, other than mine;
Till it unravels
And there's only a light smoke in my hands.

And this is where, O bed of beds!
Tiger, rough of skin and smooth of eye!
She is my loss and my lost one
And I will possess and dare, cannot possess
This other one, this similar, this One.

Like all rivers with their diverse chimes hurrying
    towards the sea,
So all my be and are towards You.
There is none but You I think of.
I know there is one thing, which is You, it is the unique
Which also in part is she,
You, not seen by her,
You, not to be reduced by my eyes' famine of her.
She and I the Rest I absorbed in You.

And well You know it; a night like this tramps off, its footsteps
small on the vast talking page it rolls its black, schoolman ruler
over, five-thousand year China and then Russia and then
Central European time, round and round and the world ac-
companied by the lights we make and the dreams closed in
our humble sleep.
Well You know it, the end I mean,
It is that by which You know the anguished communication
    between us.
Being of my being, say of my say!
We are pulled up short by death,
Our hands make the final signal on the same high-voltage wire;
    Like the mob which stampedes across a racecourse and is
    pulled up at the palisade, its members turning, regarding
    each other, surprised into violent introduction;
And I know themselves — with eye and skull, with skeleton.
As I know You, there, behind my back. As I know as far as I can
think and have thought You.

There is none so much as You, none You, I think of.

THE TOMB OF MICHAEL COLLINS

To Ignazio Silone

1

Much I remember of the death of men,
But his I most remember, most of all,
More than the familiar and forgetful
Ghosts who leave our memory too soon —
Oh, what voracious fathers bore him down!

It was all sky and heather, wet and rock,
No one was there but larks and stiff-legged hares
And flowers bloodstained. Then, Oh, our shame so massive
Only a God embraced it and the angel
Whose hurt and misty rifle shot him down.

One by one the enemy dies off;
As the sun grows old, the dead increase,
We love the more the further from we're born!
The bullet found him where the bullet ceased,
And Gael and Gall went inconspicuous down.

2
There are Four Green Fields we loved in boyhood,
There are some reasons it's no loss to die for:
Even it's no loss to die for having lived;
It is inside our life the angel happens
Life, the gift that God accepts or not,

Which Michael took with hand, with harsh, grey eyes,
He was loved by women and by men,
He fought a week of Sundays and by night
He asked what happened and he knew what was —
O Lord! how right that them you love die young!

He's what I was when by the chiming river
Two loyal children long ago embraced —
But what I was is one thing, what remember
Another thing, how memory becomes knowledge —
Most I remember him, how man is courage.

And sad, Oh sad, that glen with one thin stream
He met his death in; and a farmer told me
There was but one small bird to shoot: it sang
"Better Beast and know your end, and die
Than Man with murderous angels in his head".

3

I tell these tales — I was twelve years old that time.
Those of the past were heroes in my mind:
Edward the Bruce whose brother Robert made him
Of Ireland, King; Wolfe Tone and Silken Thomas
And Prince Red Hugh O'Donnell most of all.

The newsboys knew and the apple and orange women
Where was his shifty lodging Tuesday night;
No one betrayed him to the foreigner,
No Protestant or Catholic broke and ran
But murmured in their heart: here was a man!

Then came that mortal day he lost and laughed at,
He knew it as he left the armoured car;
The sky held in its rain and kept its breath;
Over the Liffey and the Lee, the gulls,
They told his fortune which he knew, his death.

Walking to Vespers in my Jesuit school,
The sky was come and gone; "O Captain, my Captain!"
Walt Whitman was the lesson that afternoon —
How sometimes death magnifies him who dies,
And some, though mortal, have achieved their race.

PAT BORAN

Pat Boran was born in Portlaoise in 1963. His stories and poems have been widely published. He has published one collection of his stories, "Strange Bedfellows", Salmon 1991. His first collection of poetry, "The Unwound Clock", won the Patrick Kavanagh Award and was published by The Dedalus Press in 1990.

Poetry happens at the frontiers of language. In choosing to say something in one way rather than in another, in choosing one word over another, the poet writes, updates, the history of language. He exiles and repatriates words and, in so doing, has a political and social responsibility to the world he describes. Whether or not this world seems similar to the "real world" he inhabits — the social world, the political world — makes no difference. He may, and indeed must, write for himself: but his work must also survive in the outside world.

This is not to go along with the notion that the poet is an unacknowledged legislator. Much of the time he is unaware of the processes in which he is involved. (Indeed, *if* there were a single argument for the existence of so many academy-based poetry analysts, it is that the poets themselves can seldom shed light on their own work.) Though he may opt for, or accasionally contribute to, the world of politics (by helping "to define both the language and the self-image" of his people) the usual effect of his writing is less easily discernible.

But he is not easily discouraged. The act of writing poetry might be a definition of endurance. If energy (talent aside) is what makes younger poets exciting, perseverance is what makes older poets important.

And the cliché that poetry is a religion is true only in so far as no one involved seems to have any real idea what it's all about, or where the impulse comes from. Generally it's taken on faith, or not at all.

I find it hard to be more specific. Though poems are responses to, and must survive in, the world, in sympathetic and unkind times alike they are anachronisms.

In the end it is useful only to describe them from the inside, as it were. They are children that leave home unwashed or semi-clothed. They are maps, but never of places you can return to. They are aspirations of language and feeling. They are what get written despite society — and despite poets.

- *Pat Boran*

BORN TO SHAVE

I'm so tall now at 28,
the only thing I see is my chin,
the place where my head
becomes lost in my clothes
and might be anybody's.
I look for myself in this mirror
and find only a chin, sometimes
a tooth, occasionally my tongue.

And so I wet my invisible face
like someone blind, apply, blindly,
the foam — resisting the chemical smell
until it dissipates — and bend my knees
an inch or three so that I know
it is me that I am shaving.
Born to shave.

      A child
looking in the same mirrors, I saw then
only ceiling, followed, years later,
by hints of hair, then eyes,
and then this chin. Born
to age and shave.
Born to grow up to face myself.
Born to regret and, in the light
of regret, to make promises, like this:
Years from now I'll reach
from some otherworldly place,
where none of this means anything, to touch
this hand-basin, these dulled blades.

SEVEN UNPOPULAR THINGS TO SAY ABOUT BLOOD

1
Our mothers bled, and bleed,
and our enemies,
and our enemies' mothers.

2

It rushes to the finest
nick, romances the blade.

3

It dreams
the primary dream of liquids:
to sleep, horizontally.

4

It is in the surgeon's heart,
the executioner's brain.

5

Vampires and journalists
are excited by it; poets
faint on sight.

6

I knew it better as a child,
kept scabs, like ladybugs, in jars.

7

Blood: now mine would be with yours
until the moon breaks orbit
and the nights run cold.

CHILDREN

Children in ill-fitting uniforms
drive adults to school, and children
argue the cost of tobacco
in the Newsagent's nearby.
You must have noticed them.

And in the mornings they rise to slaughter pigs,
cook breakfast, solve crosswords at the office ...
Or they send tiny adults into minefields,
barefoot, with pictures
of Khomeini around their necks,
their old toes searching the sand
for death.

And children queue for Bingo
on Ormond Quay, on Mary Street,
and douse their leaking take-aways with vinegar.

And children talk and smoke incessantly
in Eastern Health Board waiting rooms,
always moving one seat to the right,
someone's parents squabbling over trinkets
on the worn linoleum.

And it is always children
who will swear for their tobacco — children
with beards and varicose veins —
and children, dressed as policemen,
who pull their first corpses from the river.

And who is it who makes love in the dark
or in the light, who haunts
and who does all our dying for us,
if not children?

We leave their fingerprints
on everything we touch.

MODUS VIVENDI

Forget the future, your death,
the surprise on your face. Forget
everything you'll learn, too late.
Arrest the thought. What could compare
with the selflessness of plants
that mark the spot
where you will lie? If such
unthinking things can justify
the presence of the sun and planets
more completely than can you
(with all your grave considerations),
why think at all? Why squander
the irreplaceable energies? Abandon,
like some evolutionary cast-off,
this thing that brings us closest
to extinction. Forget the evidence,
the argument. Close your ears
to the debate. Forget I ever said a word —
Forget this poem.

I'LL DO IT AGAIN

1

Auld Lang Syne drifts up from downstairs.
Norma Desmond is lying on her bed,
wrists bandaged, her would-be lover
by her side to hear
her first resolution of the year:
"I'll do it again. I'll do it ... "

2

Again and again my father boomed
(pointing to broken glass,
spilt milk, or turned,
drained of colour, to the sky
where my brother's expletive still drifted
offensively towards ...):
"Will you do it again?"

My brother's predicament —
everybody's then —
was how to sound compliant
with a negative verb. As it happened
all that issued from his lips was
"I'll do it again."

3

Again and again, in places
brought into being only through
volition or resolve, MacArthur returns,
the sinner repents, the alcoholic
walks into the clean light, clean, shaven.

While elsewhere, the failing Hollywood actress
thrusts herself into imagined spotlights,
and generation upon generation of ghosts
sifts through immaculately remembered homes,
hopelessly trying to do it all, or undo it all, again.

DARK SONG

Here we are in the park
with the darkness crouched behind trees
and daylight dissolving over the city.
Something unbelievable is happening.

All day this ghost of knowledge
has whispered in my ear, all day
the very cracks in the footpath
seem significant. Something unbelievable ...

The meteor of your cigarette tip
swoops close to earth, hearth
of loving in a cold universe.
The playground swings grind their teeth

and pause. What else is there to say?
It is in our silences now, as in our voices,
that something unbelievable.
We are growing older.

WHAT HE HAS FORGOTTEN

Before the trip he checks his bags, and again
misses the fact he has forgotten it.
His mind is elsewhere — racing
ahead, frightening him with the flight path
over mountains, or the hopeful glide
above the sea. Sciences beyond him
have conspired to this achievement.
He puts his faith in history, hear-say, boyhood
experiments with kites. He must embrace
the experience of others, the statistics
of the dream...
                    Slowly, angels and tamed
monsters tend to the necessities. He follows instructions.
His bags are checked again at customs. But the officers
do not know what he has forgotten. They ascertain
what he is from what he has.
                         Aboard the plane
he discovers his address book has been left behind,
causing him to doubt not only who he is, up here,
but who, and indeed if, he has ever been.

A WORD FOR CLOUDS

In her world now six years old
there are common objects yet unnamed,
unfound in the partial vocabularies
of three homes — English,
French, Italian. *Sometimes,*
at night, the moon disappears ...

The moon disappears behind a white spot
of language. Are we shocked by this
more than by the poverty of love
given her? — this child
without clouds in her sky, *sans*
nuages, senza nubi. And
what else besides?

Try telling the young woman
she will become in six years time:
Every has a silver lining.
The will soon roll by.

BIOGRAPHY

1 The Choice of Profession

When fish speaks
  the pool records his breath
    on a thin disc
     of water which grows so large
    that it vanishes
  and the utterance is lost
in the stillness

When lion speaks
   the jungle huddles up
     in the background
       and amplifies the sound
     so it spreads
   distorted through the foliage
in the distance

When God speaks
   in the matterlessness
     in the noiselessness
       in the emptiness
       His voice is a clock
   a meter, a callipers
opposite over hypotenuse

Only scientists ever listen

2 Recollections of a Headmaster

"You know, gravity made him cry
when they told him,
and at 18 he almost
died holding Einstein's
Specific Relativity.

The *Anatomy Lesson* —
which for most is a piece
of theatre — kept him up nights,
a spectator at his neighbour's
heart bypass.

Eventually he pronounced
people independent of science,
content to leave discovery,
like power — like the future —
in the hands of a few.

Seems that microgram of knowledge
weighed like the planet on his shoulders
as though peopled by unthinking giants."

3 Science Destroys Itself

the doppler effect of footsteps
$C_8H_{10}O_2N_4$
& its response
to sugar

the notion
of a space-time continuum
while my watch semaphores
arbitrary hours

the static build-up
on inorganic material
the sector formed by
the eventual door-swing

of your exit
the white hiroshima
of that lone electron
goodbye...

HOUSE

Water clanks from the tap
like a chain. A lifetime

since anything has moved here
but rats and birds. I see

the last inhabitants as a father
and son, the father

sending the son off to the city
with a handshake and a pocket

of old pound notes.
He might as well be sending him

to bring home the time
without a watch to carry it.

CIARAN O'DRISCOLL

Ciaran O'Driscoll was born in Callan, Co Kilkenny, in 1943. He now lives in Limerick where he teaches in the School of Art and Design. He published his first collection, "Gog and Magog", in 1987 and The Dedalus Press published "The Poet and His Shadow" in 1990. In 1992 The Dedalus Press published his long poem, "The Myth of the South", (Dedalus Editions number 4). He has received a bursary in Literature from the Arts Council and was awarded the James Joyce Literary Millenium Prize in 1989.

Poetry, like charity, begins at home, but it shouldn't end there. My poetic voyage has tried to steer a course between the Scylla of the poet as civil servant, who is simply an extension of the State's apparatus into the realm of myth-making, and the Charybdis of the uninvolved poet, who regards his work as an entity-in-itself, unbesmirched by, and unresponsible for, the world in which it was born.

I don't believe that poetry presents an alternative to the world; it is part of the world, and comes into its own bearing the indelible birthmarks of the sorrow and joy of living. My hope for the poetry *I* write is that it will be read by those who are committed to the world rather than by those who want to escape into a pure realm of aesthetics. But that is not to say that I don't take aesthetics seriously, only that my aesthetics are not etherial.

For example, I believe in using the word *garage* in a poem, but I will try to use it in such a way that it is part of a general aesthetic texture, while it still *refers* inescapably to something in the world that is oily and smelly but ultimately good in some sense because it exists.

I believe that poetry has every right to comment on the social and the political, but that a political statement is not necessarily a poem *per se*, any more than is a statement about so-called "poetical" subjects such as love and trees. Anything can be handled in poetry, as long as it is handled poetically. It is also worth remembering that poetry is unpredictable; critics say it is one thing and it turns out to be another.

I also believe that poetry should "defamiliarize" the ordinary, and familiarize the exotic and esoteric. The ultimate drive of my poetry is, I think, towards a sense of the inter-relatedness of many things and many levels.

- *Ciaran O'Driscoll*

ANATOMY OF THE COPPER MAN

(copperwork figure seen in a pub, West of Ireland)
The entry wound is under the right elbow - here.
And as you can see
the neck of the fiddle has struck the heart. In fact
almost the whole fiddle has entered the body.
Only the head and feet remain intact.

Each arm, each leg is fifteen fragments;
the trunk an archipelago, a jigsaw
presided over by the moonstruck face.

A relic of *geansaí* adheres to the neck;
lapels of a vanished coat. A straw hat
crowns this extraordinary apparition.
It fidgets forward in fine copper boots,
its own backbone for walking stick.

A king of shreds and patches, gentlemen,
held together by no thread of consequence.
Note how the fixed grin belies
the fact that the night sky floats through the wounds.

THE TREE OUTSIDE MY WINDOW

There are many mansions in
the tree outside my window.

James Joyce is there, reciting
the sequel to *Finnegans Wake*
to oysters eating fillets of the rich
in its seafood restaurant,

and there's the repentant Pope
nodding in total agreement
with the Marxist theologians
of its leafy constellations.

And the cringing olive-eyed
mongrel from down the lane
takes the evening paper
from his former master's mouth,

while the children of Peru
throw away their begging bowls
and screaming with delight
climb to the topmost branches.

O the fine ales the beautiful dead
drink in the tree outside my window!

Green is its darkness, and its silver
in the breeze is starlight.

GREAT AUKS

The great auk is an extinct bird
that keeps on laying eggs;
and the more eggs it lays,
the more extinct it becomes.

The eggs, as soon as they are laid,
are put in glass cases in museums,
where egg-reviewers look at them, and say:
"This is the best egg yet
from this particular great auk,
we look forward to the next."

All the eggs of all the extinct great auks
in the world are exactly the same shape and size,
pages upon pages of them,
and if you placed them end to end,
they would circle the globe many times,
and there's more coming.

It's not easy to become a great auk,
you must first become extinct
so that the quality of extinction
can be transmitted to the eggs you lay.

Great auks don't speak to other birds,
and since they can't fly
they have founded a Great Auk Society
to declare flying unfashionable,

and all other birds that wish to become great auks
must consent to have their wings clipped
by the Great Auk Society,
and meditate, night and day,
on the virtue of great aukness.

Eventually, they'll lay
eggs of the correct shape and size,
scarcely noticing that in the process
they have become extinct.

NIGHT PORTER

Chiselled in black, a lioness
couchant on both sides of the staircase
neither keeps watch nor falls asleep.

The night porter conspires to keep
the obsequies of a gangster from eyes
under a dome window of stained glass
in motifs of flowers and fruit,
from guests who are sitting down to eat
a sea-bed served on ice. Platefuls
of empty crustacean shells
are carefully removed by waiters.

Meanwhile, the pensive night porter
is interrupted in his trains
of thought to phone an ambulance
for a call girl injured in bondage,
to go upstairs and disengage
young lovers who sneaked to a room.

The dancers are leaving the ballroom,
the lobby brightens with evening dress.

The night porter's face is expressionless.

SMOKE WITHOUT FIRE

"I see smoke without fire," declared
the old man in the flapping tent,
"but when the thickening smoke will stand
aside for flame I cannot say.

"It has happened many times before
that I have suffered needlessly
from expectation when the sky
grew dark with smoky messengers.

"Smoke has set me apart
and sent me to live on this hill.
I am punished for smoke like a child
who cannot build a fire.

"Down in the kraal, where things have stayed
as they were in the beginning,
dogs bark when I beg for bread,
smoke-alarms blink in taverns."

Thus cryptically spoke
the old man in the flapping tent
who could not make the future flame
when he stood aside from the present.

ROONEY'S MOUTH

Rooney, the cat, has swallowed my past
and is sleeping it off on the sofa.
I'd like to recover a few small pieces
before digestion begins in earnest,
but I baulk at the thought of explaining
a disembowelled cat when my wife comes home.

A different theory says that I should comb
the Dock Road in our red Sentra tonight,
since all the other women I've ever loved
have become prostitutes from sheer despair
of realizing what they lost in me.

And through the mornings and afternoons,
they sleep in wretched bedsitters, watched over
by the Sacred Heart and his perpetual lamp,
courtesy of pious but unsuspecting
landladies who won't mend their leaking roofs.

There's one piece of the very recent past
I'm so insanely hooked on, I'm afraid
the sofa may be shortly soaked in blood.
I can't think of a plausible excuse
to visit the Dock Road tonight:

the famous fishmonger closed at five,
and smoked salmon and lobsters crammed in tanks
so tightly they have scarcely room to writhe
and prove to customers they're still alive
and shelled prawns and fillets of hake and sidelines
in woodcock and grouse fell into Rooney's Mouth.

THE GARDEN OF POSSIBLE FUTURES

In the garden of possible futures,
there's no question of profundity
or guilt in the broadest sense,
though there may be some reason
why the gardener sprinkles his boots.

While Catriona phones for a taxi,
a languor of plums and peaches
wounds the heart of a great angler
who crucially lacks assertiveness,

a great angler of plums and peaches
who sprinkles his boots in the depths
of the garden of possible futures.

While Catriona waits for a taxi,
her father, another great angler,
a motionless pike in the drawing room,
will drink a post-prandial brandy.

No question here of profundity
or guilt in the broadest sense.
In the depths of the garden of possible futures,
Catriona hears lullabies in her nightmares.

IN OREGON

(for Ger Killeen and Kate Saunders)

1.
If you could speak of a town ten miles long
as being hemmed in, then Lincoln City was,
between the Pacific and the forest hills
of Oregon: "Ten miles of hotdog stalls",
as Kate, herself an Oregonian,
described the hastily-improvised look
of that long street, a wild-west city made
from the meeting up of several wild-west towns.

So now you drive, rather than walk, to showdowns.

2.
And the Lincoln City post office assistant
was straight out of *American Gothic*
(which I saw later in Chicago):
a dour fundamentalist without her pitchfork,
but for all I knew she had hidden it
under the counter and would impale

heretics who believed in such things
as the International Express Mail;
and when the computer proved her orthodox,
I worried about unseen prongs.

3.

The house is surrounded by hills
of Hemlock and Douglas Fir,
and on a platform outside
at night, a pair of raccoons clamber
for scattered food, wearing their burglar's masks,
their bushy tails striped like a convict's suit.
Bowing and scraping across the stage
in a fearful instinctive dance,
they gather up peanuts and lift them
to eat in cupped miniature hands
like humans drinking water from a spring,
actors acknowledging an ovation,
blowing kisses to a delirious night
of bears, coyotes, mountain lions,
and drunken redneck loggers poised to shoot
at roadsigns, guns protruding from their holsters.

4.

And a gun protruded from the holster
of a wild-eyed logger in blue denim
I saw striding among Safeway consumers
who were meekly carrying Easter provisions
from store to car: *what is he looking for,*
this tall wild-eyed cowboy in blue?

Have I stepped into a Western?

5.

And the radio says the Blazers have won
again, and further down the coast,
in Los Angeles, the police have been
caught red-handed on video at last
beating a black traffic offender senseless,

and I'm peering through dim binoculars
from the veranda of Kate's mother's house,
watching a darker smudge on the bottle-
green of the end-of-March Pacific
that might turn out to be a killer whale.

6.
And finally, those land-cousins
of yellow waterflowers
I photographed with my cheap camera
beside Slab Creek in twilight downpours,

the spring bloom of a weed
called Skunk Cabbage, in the field
near the children's school founded
by ageing Hippies: the shot that failed.

MARGARITAS

In some arty-decor friendly-neighbourhood sidestreet
not far from the John Hancock Centre towering
over Chicago at Michigan and Chestnut,
a horse of a different colour in the uncertain sunshine
of an early April afternoon, I drank Margaritas:
tequila tang met salt tang of the glasses rim
on my lips, a silver sun at the world's end.

Salt tang and tequila, bite of lime and cold of ice,
and the husky voice of a plump but petite waitress:
"Why d'ya wanna *buy* food, when it's *complimmenary?*"
Hot chilli sauce on Buffalo chicken wings, in Chicago,
the friendly-neighbourhood voices of people who greet
one another every day, young white women bantering
with black men, and the occasional cadaverous
eyes of a down-and-out watching across the way
and waiting for eye-contact to encourage him
to come and introduce his needs at the railing
that separates the sidewalk from the tables
of Margarita-drinkers outside a Mexican café
on a street that runs parallel with Lake Shore Drive,
where I among them, conscious of the towering height
of the John Hancock Centre, Chestnut St., a horse
of a different colour, am sinking into silver light,
tequila and salt meeting at the world's rim.

JOHN JORDAN

John Jordan was born in Dublin in 1930. He had a distinguished career as university lecturer, reviewer, theatre critic, broadcaster. He published some small collections of his verse during his lifetime. After his untimely death in 1989 Poolbeg published his collected stories, and in 1991 The Dedalus Press published his "Collected Poems", edited by Hugh Mc Fadden. McFadden wrote: "Mr Jordan's stature as a poet has not been fully appreciated yet — except by those peers among his contemporaries who were secure enough in the knowledge of their own talent not to feel any jealous sense of rivalry regarding Mr Jordan's undoubted abilities: writers such as Patrick Kavanagh, Austin Clarke, Pearse Hutchinson; or else by those younger poets who blossomed in the halcyon days in the Sixties when John Jordan was editing *Poetry Ireland*, when he had 'the blinds up and the door on the latch' ".

For all John Jordan's sense of fun, and there is undoubtedly a wilfulness about much that he wrote, there is a common factor apparent throughout, a seriousness of purpose. The range of subjects is finally antic, but is part of the serious record of a complex and erudite individual obsessed with the connections — the Baudelairean *correspondances* — of things. He wrote his poems to the occasion and for the occasion as it arose, but always seized the opportunity to consider the wider implications, the sometimes apparently unresolvable implications, of being a human being and remaining a human being, and yet, somehow, not being deluded. A deeply religious man, a "Catholic in the European sense" who on more than one occasion noted that Hope is hard, he also brought a tough Protestant rigour to bear on his lifelong application to the problems of faith and forgiveness, and in this he could, and did, call on the traditions of Bunyan. To be a pilgrim, in this tradition, in itself has grace, is worth the candle, and with Bunyan he believed passionately in the necessity of seeking out salvation.

..... John Jordan was, quite simply, one of the most loveable people I have ever known. Those who knew him well will need no reminding, those who did not will have to take it on faith. Though not entirely on faith, there are, after all, the poems, the hundreds of thousands of words of literary journalism, the critical pieces, the short stories, the radio broadcasts, the writings of those whom he was the first to edit, encourage and publish. There are the literary magazines dotted matter-of-factly about the country, and the small presses turning out a healthy sum of books each year, and a greater public understanding of the place of literature in our lives. All in all, it i s a better scene than that which confronted him as a young writer in the fifties, and the improvements are due in no small part to him.

- Macdara Woods
from the introduction to John Jordan's "Collected Poems"

NOTES FOR AN OBSCENE SEQUENCE

The silver fox, my darling,
Will gobble up your breast,
O strip yourself, come quick with me,
Be naked, that's the test.

Our trees of iron are just as fine
As shoots of flowering shrubs,
The martinis of my kisses
As good as gin in pubs.

You'll soon forget the pleasure-trips
To Mayo or Shanghai,
But in the end you'll always feel
My hand upon your thigh.

So throw away the chicken-legs,
Come fasten on my mouth,
And when you're glutted there, my bird,
We'll take a trip down South.

ELEGIAC NOTES ON R.C.

1

Robert has made an exhibition of himself.
He has passed over to the decent people,
Struck a bargain with the blessed,
And the beasts in Leeson Street are mourning:
Several fellows incontinently grieved
And a couple of women who knew the truth.
O Robert among the saints
Give us your paradiction.

2

The morning before Robert's exhibition
A woman looked down, not at Kinsella's
    "Baggot Street Deserta"
But on a wide tawny desert
Where there is no Gaulle but only simplicities:
A woman washing
Beyond the lintels.

A GUEST OF THE DEAN'S

for Austin Clarke

1.

Great Dean, invigilator of our loves and liberties,
Here is United Ireland. The burrs of thirty-two counties
Stick in my heart. That cool twelve thou' has
Bought me fraternity. We are all experts here.
Schizophrenics, depressives, alcoholics, pathics,
Some elated like the Blessed Saints, others
Withdrawn to who knows what red hell or
Candid heaven, all are duly elected members,
Academicians who may never resign, signatories
Of the treatment.
                    Woe to the formulators of empty oaths.
They may know again the quality of shipwreck,
Watch with eyes like piss-holes in the snow
Manannán betray his tasty kinship with Moloch,
Be trapped at Calais by the mad Irishwoman
Who thinks she lives among niggers: sniggers
Should be the rhyme. Madness is no laughing
Matter. Though some here laugh like madmen.
                    In remote farms tongueless bachelors
Stash barley and juniper against demonic thirst.
Forget their caches and drive mad through
St. Patrick's snakeless night. The sheebeen is
Mother's arms. The paps are horny
With plenty. The cocks crow. Swollen

Teats are dumb. Last night their
Master was "fierce lonely".
             "Have you a drinking problem?"
"Well, I suppose, like the other lads." Your
Toms, Dicks and Harrys are here, great Dean.
You gave your lolly to found our first democratic
Institution. Paudeen and Algernon rub minds.

2.

Some who have gone from soft to hard
Have been warned by Nurse against lonely pathic.
The Eye of Heaven blazes on the strollers
in the Gardens of *Welldorm:* did the bats
Come in middle of night? The cats tie themselves
To your body? The scimitars castrate you?
The *Artane* Band parades among the roses.
The Legion of *Gardenal* inspects the dahlias.
(Great Dean, your people, yours and mine,
          call them day-lias).
Surmontilised, the clock-golfers beat the rap.
Cuchullains, tight-pantsed, hand the ball,
Mini-skirted Deirdres ply the racquet.
They do not pray for you at Mass, great Dane,
As your people called you.
                         When the Host is raised
They think not of your Liberties or Loves,
Each soul dead-set for personal salvation
Accepts as natural bounty your crazed wish,
Forgets the torment in the ears and heart,
Would surely damn a man with two women.
                    Our democracy has its fascists.
The love of man and man is "dirt". Among the
Roses and the dahlias as the all-seeing Eye
Blinks alight I'm told it's "worse than besti-itis".
(A notable coinage from the County of Laois.)
                         At Courtown on holiday
Ex-inmates meet. Do they discuss
Heights of *Valium,* Scrolls of *Librium* or
Those strolls in the Gardens of *Welldorm?*

3.

United Ireland has its constipation problems.
Immemorial castor oil still has its uses.
Some of our citizens like Martin, Francois, yourself
                                        great Dane,
Make us privy to their cloacal mysteries.
Bowels without compassion confuse thought,
Spanner the works: pique, bad temper!
                        All the rage is regularity.
The men on the Moon must be punctual.
Many will bay if poet's image is violated
While *Welldorm* or *Doriden* is in the saddle.
Insomniacs, inviolate to patent sleep, will
Bless their sickness if they catch the telly
While others dream of Bacchus' sloppy lips,
Ganymede's slim-fit hips, Venus' abounding bosom.
                        To-morrow our democracy
Will drop marmalade, slobber porridge,
Let fry cool, tea tar, valued butt incinerate.
We are all experts here. Elated and withdrawn
Will find the Moon their common ground.
Boozers will start out of pre-planned temptation,
The sick of Eros will goggle at heart's craters revealed.
You, great Dane, chained on your parthogenetic rock,
May remember when the Moon had its liberties,
When the Liberties had a Moon and a Man in it.
Pray for us, reluctant Prometheus. Remember
The House of which you are Father.

(St Patrick's Hospital, founded by Jonathan Swift)

HEIMWEH

To have *Heimweh* for a madhouse
To half-hear Jaime when he discusses Sender
(Chiefly *cosas amorosas y sexuales*)
To in short be a member of an institution

200

For medicated vegetables, is not a solid preparation
For the infrequent 16A and the price of vegetables,
I mean vegetables for real, the moulting cauliflower,
The lecherous carrot, the hearted cabbage,
The mosquish onion, the shrewish radish,
All the bounty men dig in plots,
Not excluding the unchaste celery,
And the parsnip made famous by Yeats,
Whose *Heimweh* for Inisfree is pretty suspect.
But then one suspects them all,
Du Bellay, Donncha Rua, whoever
Was responsible for "Galway Bay" frightening
Manannán on the way to Liverpool,
Dread accompaniment to puke and puddle,
The heart of exile stinking of stale stout:
Porter had a Synge to it but not bottled
Inclement stout that loosens liver and lights.
Ah the relief of Liverpool and the great clock tower.
There are thousands and thousands who've had *Heimweh*
      for Liverpool
But to have it for a madhouse is at least invidious,
To love fiercely the faces of the violently unhappy,
Rhoda the hippopotamus whose daughter's a bitch,
Young snapper who's handy at his wrists,
Minds with just that one mote in them,
The thread that coarsens the turnip:
Such love is certifiable, the lover a fink,
A mind pickled with Gaelic salads,
Unchristian sauces, unfree libations
Fit for Romany, Lascar, Pink,
But surely not for one whose hand
Has cracked the ice in the Holy Water stoup,
Who has stooped and crackled muscles
Before the Ark of the Most High;
But, saving thought: whatever of Him was man
Decidedly was finkish; our iconologists
Depict him long-haired, he lay about
Not only in the Garden, went in for love-feasts,
Suffered the ministrations of tarts. His Father
Put him through most drastic therapy:
At a time like that, resurrectionary thoughts were not,

I'd say, a balsam.
So in all, perhaps He would countenance
Heimweh for a madhouse, humanly speaking
Prefer Rhoda the hippopotamus whose daughter's a bitch,
jack-o'-the-Blade who is handy at his wrists,
And something tells me all those motes,
Collective maculae, might make a beam
That would sustain a sane world, my masters,
And utilise Spandau for peevish purposes.

Who'd be sent there, and by whom, is matter for another poem.

FOR JULIUS HENRY MARX (1891 - 1977)

Among the blazing azaleas
Of the Parque del Campo Grande
I perceived the true, sophisticated
Marxist point of view:
Let the people have duck soup;
Let them at the races lose their shirts,
let them shirtless storm the Opera,
And stop the shrieks of Mimi with Coronas.
Chiefly, let them raise intemperate eyebrows
To the infinite spaces of the stars.

(Valladolid-Madrid, August/September 1977)

TO Ms MAE WEST ON HER 85th

What right have you?
Did you pat your platinum alps
When across the electric wire
The thrilling message came
That the pelvic muscles were tranquillized
The gluteal shivers forever fridged
That in fact (O lamentable extinction!)
Elvis had gone pop?

Or did you cable another Cadillac
To some lucky mother-doll of Christ's
Or over caskets run your pensive eye,
Golden, placid, lined with peachy silk,
And have your Self remeasured
For the last tango with the beautician
Who'll set all curves in proper mould,
The plastic dugs on top?

I weep not for the King: he wasn't my type.
(Well, give him some pink, false roses.)
But you, old timer, had better go West
While the pickings (pan me a nugget, Beulah)
Are ripe. The blue jeans of yesteryear
Might yet reverence your mummy,
And e'en their grassed spawn be mesmerized.

MICHEAL

25 October 1899 - 6 March 1978

Doffed the curious toupées
Unflaked the valorous *maquillage*
    A pale olive haze
    On special days
    As when Lennox
    Going to the Ball
    Plastered his face green
    For no reason at all

The great player relaxes
(Does he smoke a Celtique?)
Waits for this ultimate call.
"O what will people say?"

In a sub-tropical garden
Drenched in moonlight
Moths, midges, white butterflies,
Die on my cheeks
As I cry for you.

LOLEK

Czestochowa, Jasna Gora — Auschwitz, Nova Huta:
Archdiocese Cracow:
Symphony of ashed flesh and steel and Mary,
Uncountable dark nights in the factory of death,
Salvos of laud on the Black Virgin's White Mountain,
The people of God keen from metal with metamorphosed hearts
Expectancy and rose of Christ's fair state
You have known it all:
Grease-paint, desk, sledge-hammer,
Arc-light, explosive, grammar,
Mickiewicz's mighty line,
More resounding than Wagnerian microphones,
Juliusz Slowacki in the Szkackas' drawingroom,
Promethean Cyprian Norwid,
Poor Zegladlowicz who pained the clergy
And Juan de la Cruz wrestling,
Parched in a tawny landscape,
With the Angel of Faith.

You expect much faith from Patrick's children.
In this our pleasant land of Country and Western singers,
So great a hope as yours must find it.
And meantime — while the phones ring
    and the keys tap and the words spawn —
Let the chisellers and the unstained
Sing a carol for Karol:
"May Holy Ireland be holier,
Perhaps even made whole".

JOHN ENNIS

John Ennis won the Patrick Kavanagh Award in 1975. He has published several collections of his poetry and has been represented in many anthologies. He lives in Co Waterford and works as head of Humanities in Waterford RTC. In 1990 The Dedalus Press published "Arboretum", a long poem by John Ennis which was the prizewinning work at Listowel Writers' Week in that year. In 1991 The Dedalus Press published his collection "In a Green Shade".

Narrative informs my work, poems often being mini-stories, jibbing at the constraints of "verse", sometimes calling on the archetype. I am drawn also to the persona, while aware of the caveats of M. Holub. The persona makes possible a dialectic (the later Yeats found it useful) in a land where the real dialectic of communities, the "jaw-jaw" has not even begun. "The Croppy Boy" and "Alice of Daphne" are examples.

While acknowledging the New Narrative in the US in the eighties, I grew up with the tradition anyway (I got a present of the collected Milton at fifteen). The earliest poems I kept returning to were "The Great Hunger", "Zima Junction" and "The Quaker Graveyard at Nantucket". I once had all of the latter off by heart.

The poems make comment on collective experience by attempting to focus on particular details of that experience. The "interior" landscape is of less importance than that of the larger community, or communities. The narrator is witness as well as participant. The locale is identifiable to the insular psyche. The res publica is never too far away. In *Arboretum* I set about felling, clearing and replanting the interior landscape for a new international. Given the basic tenets here of a shared christianity, the problem remains as ever to apply them. The narrator sees the death of a British soldier on our soil as an obscenity. Why should Ghandi have all the kudos?

Ultimately nobody is an observer. Is not everyone "a walker/from the knees down?".

I admit little sympathy with that effete nihilism one notes in passing, the quasi-lyrical narcissistic whimper, the brilliant self-conscious carapace of the fine volume, where the real song is Plato's ghost and heavy metal. This is not to denigrate the truly "personal" serving as guide to everyperson. The poems that helped to shape Stasi-land, too, fell off the hungry presses in scattered leaves. I admit, also, a certain rage as a promoter of education, addressing the masses of the bright young mesmerised by choice of the largely non-existent, the dubious, a less-than-bridled capitalism.

As for prosody, give me a supple blank verse line, or free verse where the snatched cadences of the King James

(Alice of Daphne) can serve as well as the modern idiom.

Of late the poems tend to work "the poetic line" rather than "the prose sentence". The rhythm is marked (since it is synonymous with movement) and so time is marked. Understatement, or its opposite, allows a resident tension. The nature and role of the artistic act is a preoccupation, in Orpheus and "Watching the Descent of Yuichiro Miura". I feel a greater affinity with Thrace (that other extreme of Celtdom) than with any "free" and cultured Athena.

I exult in the verse of contemporaries and its variety from the presses. I am equally entranced with Wang Wei organising poetry competitions on his melon patch, the last poets of imperial Rome, or the South Korean, Pak Tu-jin, contemplating today in two hundred works the creative power in water-washed stones. For history, there's more than enough in Joseph Lee, our cancerous nationalism, and the colour-blindness of the flag-facing masses.

- John Ennis

AENGUS ON ARAN

1 Morning, and I head out to Aran, the old disarray,
See once more your ocean-spattered battlements, Aengus,
Cheerless the herds of the young, gruel of the day,
Justice the alien hand of the stone god feeds us:

Hemmed in, hundreds with wounds, the keen wolfhounds,
    the grey
Grassroots on the rock wait for the signal to build, the word
Of hope. Otherwise they'll fall, rot too in the seal-dead bay.
Crabs on the Atlantic floor will strike the bitter chord.

Stone. Bronze. Iron. Lives pass. The tears of an infant.
Your cauldron fires lie unlit. Gold. Glass. Metallurgy.
Wood dwindles. Forage stone for roots, the edible plant.

Cliffs, to the sunset, drop sheer. Poet, from this height
No retreat is possible. The same mad poor-mouthed sea
Licks your hurt in the irrigated, unscrupulous light.

2   Yes! Home to the Atlantic! The true salt on our cheeks.
For it is no fluke that here you ordered stone on stone,
Firmed chevaux-de-frise bedrock. Now in future weeks
You'll build of our beleagured wills that final bastion.

The green plains are lost to your children. Firbolgs enshrine
The emerald flicker at their fingertips, the robotic gall
Of the breadline. Industry opens with cheese and wine.
See, here, the narrow door of rock for the hounded animal.

Sailing west, you settled for extremity. With eyes of pride
You choose our last outpost. Stand armed. Youngsters
      mend a net.
In the damp cantankerous dawn wives scold and chide.

We'll fish from dizzy elevations down into the low sunset.
Like snow in winter sea foam drifts along Aran at high tide.
I see skins grow lousy. Bodies are shivering in the wet.

3   Mount the sentries! The coin hoarders of ordure and ease
School the Croms of the boyish fields, would make us kneel
To them, Aengus. Impossible. Though we know no release,
House us with polity and poems fit to quieten the desolate seal.

Friends didn't make it this far. The best fell in their bogs
      with the acorn.
You wait as fanatical as the legendary thin Eleazar ben Jair.
The first snow falls early on warm generations, the not yet born,
And on love, and lovers, not yet cradled to breathe clean air.

We'll perfect sea-craft, sail your combers in the rain.
Snatch soil from crevices to pluck the yearly morsel,
Snatch eggs from screaming gulls to still the pain,

Wait on the moon-lit ramparts, construct your twelve-foot walls
For as long as it takes. I fear wild summers we cannot haul
The blue shark in, much less boil livers, extract the oils.

ENVOI

The lamps are going out. Fear rages, epidemic. There remains
    this sky
And this rock. And the ocean with gulls and geese. Some fish
    to get by.
Soon the last wave. Guide us well, Aengus, in tomorrow's
    strategy.

THE CROPPY BOY

It's no use, your wild nightly haggle, horse-pissed over me
At Passage by the Suir or maudlin down in Duncannon stoned.
The piked suns shine on ever more cruelly watery.
Winy streets we littered are innocently crimsoned.

On wet cobbles to the sweaty rope, you'll halo me. Naïve,
O yes, my blond teenage hair is styled like the French.
I'm not crying. To ladies, prance of Hessians, I clench
My body dream, walk on. My ignorant head's a bee-hive.

From their suite rooms the yogurt mouths of hypocrites
Spit me out like bile. No lusty Patrick sucks their tits.

Rousing Christ, ladies do with me what they please.
While I die, blackbirds sing up the fat-arsed trees.

Mother. It's cruel, Yeomen bar us any last good-bye.
Yesterday I danced, tapped a jig. Noon, see me die.

ALICE OF DAPHNE, 1799

I am Alice of Daphne, and my heart clogs for John Pounden.
  As the stag cornered by pitch-forks, so antlered his thought
against the Croppies.
  As the Jonathan amongst scented trees of the orchard, so rose
my sweet back in Daphne. I knew a tender spot down under
his branches, basked long among his juicy apples.

 He rushed me the road to Enniscorthy. I was far gone,
awkward with our loving:
  Bed me with slovens, madden me with fiddles, I grow
big now, sick for Daphne.
  His trunk leant gently onto mine, for I was fourteen
years of age.

                               *

  And I said, Never. Never shall we be torn asunder or cut
off from petalled Daphne, though our green hills crawl back
with Croppies like flies, for I will not unloose that daft
chase wreathing our laurels up the sloped white blossoms.
  I grafted and shall graft, Jonathan, my virgin bones
to yours.
  McGuire, good tenant, coffined you when we stank
Enniscorthy where Croppies piked the brave Orange.

 John was twenty-one under the fruiting tree. I played
the skittery dove after his apples.
  Look, my lovelies, the mason plumbs our Wall! You can
walk by the Slaney!
  Crocus open on the Spring Lawn. On Vinegar Hill
Providence stooped and smiled and picked but a few
of the Croppies.

The Black Prince plum blooms early this March
for my dears, Mary, John Colley, Jane, Patrick, Fanny.
But poor baby Joshua is down with the fits.

LONDONDERRY

'88

As long as the Foyle rises, the eagle flies
and heather blooms for the late bell honey
this black acid soil is for living in.
Peninsulas are ample with their grain,
Hazels with their catkins give us nuts.
We are afraid you will take them from us.
You do not have sole rental on these oaks
and that is why I close the gates on you.

Antrim, why do you think so bad of us?
Our hearts beat to the same rhythms,
our children go to school like yours
but you have cut them from our wombs
served up young boys to their fathers
fed us in tears to the swollen rivers.
The same bad blood now races both our veins
and that is why I close the gates on you.

Was there not one corner you could have spared?
Was there not one field we could have bargained
shaking hands across wheat, wished a blessing
on like neighbours over intestate green fences?
If a forgotten polity brought our mothers
why grind on their sons such bitter querns?
Deep down you call on us little but evil
and that is why I close the gates on you.

Both our fathers, too, were once seafarers.
If we look to London, why do you rage?
"Irish", were you so planted from Adam?
Intruders, we both sailed west to furze-lit hills,
like you, we dug dykes, sowed corn, threw up roofs;
like you we had dreams, strong limbs, girls we craved.
I love the full harvest moon too over the Creggan
and that is why I close the gates on you.

I have no illusions,
the men I fight are young like me
goaded by old dotards and their bells.
You do not question,
you do not isolate the plumed wolves
you do not weep when my friends die
you do not
and that is why I close the gates on you.

Do not feed me with your dead heroes.
For me every perch of earth is sacred,
every rood is a bounty from creation.
If there were the sun, I would grow you figs.
If there were the sun, I would give you wine.
If there were the sun, I would sell you olives.
I'm not enchanted by your mythic vapours
and that is why I close the gates on you.

Old Windbags, do not treat us to your tares
for you have wiped us off this fair island.
Christ, at our backs lies the pirate fleet!
But I know you will be merciless and wind
our guts, like Brodar's, round your trees.
We have our stones and scythes and pikes
here for you have made of us the masters
and that is why I close the gates on you.

Daybreak, tomorrow, I'll eat the same gruel
back to the grind of the apprentice
hammering till the salt sweat trickles
as the frosty bosses lord it over our souls.
We are not the first, or the last poor
squabblers across white tussocks in the blood.
We have full right like you to this blue December sky
and that is why I close the gates on you.

WATCHING THE DESCENT OF YUICHIRO MIURA

first to ski down the top of Everest

Miura, alone in a tent of candles, desolate at heart
You wait for dawn on Everest, the challenge of Icarus.
World champion, skier of the fastness of our high sky
Your meekness is etched forever on the peerless glacier.

O pilgrim, these high peaks pirate away your identity
As the frigid pavilion of the mountain becomes a tomb.
Brain cells deteriorate. All the warm human senses dull.
Ice walls lighten to pools of silver in the western coomb.

At these heights, a universe of silence. Imagination is
Eclipsed and the mind exhausts the last squirrel stores
Of cognisance. At twenty thousand feet, the south coll
Trails its royal plumes of snow down to the jet stream.
Yesterday, on your last trial, a loss of consciousness:
Parachute on the sacred sheer like an airy lotus blossom.
The frozen dome was too brittle even for the brave Sherpas.
One died. But guides would not allow you call off the climb.

213

The Himalayan partridge spreads her wings many miles
    below
Where meadowed valleys speak with rivulets, honeyed wells.
Up here, the ozone is no more than a stone's throw
From Yeats's cold fisherman by his river in the hills.
The grey guinea-pigs of industry this morning at home
Motor the daily labyrinths of steel, tooth and claw.
This older firmament holds the same vitreous chrome.
Frozen outcrops jut up as tall as ten Liberty Halls.

Higher, where the Swedes stopped, two thousand cold feet
From the actual summit, you ascend totally at your ease.
The day is eerie with freezing. Grit of névé blasts cheek
Bones. Zero here is tropical. The icebox never thaws.
Oxygen starts to sing, deeper now, rehearsed in your lungs.
You're so high the sky is blackening! Crevasses crowd
Commonplace! One false step on the fickle snow of words...
Peaks are puny abutments into a dark deep nothingness.

Blur! Hunch of granular! You are off! Ski the glacier, —
Attempt the unknown packed aeons of our primal Everest,
Hug her rock-strewn slalom. Your split-second diagonals
Confirm a hold on the white Pegasus of the mountain!
If arms were wings you would be Greek, daring Icarus.
The earth and sky are yours and God's white thigh of myth.
You play with the ondes martinou every frenzy of style
Redeeming all prose voices buried deep in the ancient rime.

Poet, with a plummeting of skis, steel nerve, leaden skies
You somersault. Sherpas of dismay strike out for your body's
Mad cascade just halted at the black rock, the white abyss.
Telescopic eyes rivet on your soul where you lie unharmed.
As you weep, I think of those few humans to court greatness,
Embrace your humility and courage beneath the pewter sky
And your noble art shooting the last rapids of space,
Apices of ice to whose state you bring illumination.

214

Miura, you had feared the old gods of the sun,
Moon, and the far off white extinguishable stars
As fated as those colourful Tibetan villagers
Begging you to join their dance at a festival.
You walk down from a high wind crying in summer,
From the cairn of thanks you built the Mountain,
Child of the Sea, altar with a mirror to honour
Her, beautiful among her sisters at the top of the world.

THE TREE OF MAN

on the death of Patrick White

I walked into your clearing then. The trees had thinned —
Obscure scrub, briar in my path, and the not understood
Lifted and the light, the sunlight was excruciating,
To be greatful for. Fruit lit every tree in that wood.

I cried in that clearing. My life lay in your chosen words.
When I panicked in the centre of the field with the stream
Rattling at the end, there were your pages only to return to.
I put one rooted foot in front of the other, one at a time.

Struggled back for Amy, the rag and bone of Sarsaparilla
In bloom, *Down at the Dump*, the greatest story ever told,
Stan Parker, who found faith in a garden of withered cabbages,
Crumbs you ate with Manoly scouring many a church fold.

Asthmatic, you sat all night, waiting for a cure
Writing *The Tree* at a table, each leaf a torture.

from ARBORETUM

Philip is gone. We dawdle. Just ourselves.
Paths with Latin roots fork into the trees.
Borges disappears amid whitebeam for centuries.
The air is warm. Workmen are returning.
On Carrickbyrne Hill bracken is burning.
Prime pollen time. And the bees
Hum on the cotoneaster trees.

"I hope he'll be all right".

"What harm can befall him?"

No greater than when thorn-caught
Among the ornamental robus,
The arching white-washed bramble
From Central China, — he'd gone for its snowy
Blossoming; — or, barefoot, like a lemur
Hanging on some graceful robinia, break the brittle
Tree: the rose acacia from the Americas
Lobe-pendent and fragrant as sweet-pea flowers.
He'll know most of them off by heart and touch.
Theirs a shudder under him less than a loved
One's soon: robinia viscosa, clammy locust
Or the South Allegheny Mountain acacia.
Child, you'll be pocketing snowberries,
Coral berries, the ones the birds have not fed on,
Scattered rich with random seed across the land.

LELAND BARDWELL

Leland Bardwell grew up in Leixlip, Co Kildare. She has lived in London, Paris, and Dublin. At present living in County Monaghan. She went to school in Dublin and later studied Ancient History in London University as an extra-mural student. She has given poetry readings all over Ireland, France, Hungary and England. She was awarded a creative writing bursary by the Irish Arts Council in 1978 and again in 1980. She has worked as a translator in Paris and Budapest. She is also a novelist and a playwright. In 1991 The Dedalus Press published her new and selected poems, "Dostoevsky's Grave".

In a poem by Agnes Nemes Nagy she talks about a bird on her shoulder. By coincidence I have always imagined a similar phenomenon. There has always been a bird on my shoulder. As a child I was frightened of birds, afraid of their brittle bones, their hot beating hearts, their own terror of me; perhaps that is why my subconscious produced this bird. It is black, its plumage is dull, its wings droop, its beak hangs down as though it slept. I don't know what kind of bird it is — perhaps a cross between a blackbird and a crow, nothing out of the ordinary. It has been known to sit quiet for months and then, without warning, it wakes up, flutters, scratches, starts pecking at the side of my head. That is when the poems come. Sometimes one after the other, day after day. It is the black comedy of life without which we — or I, at least, would be powerless to prevent myself from spinning off the whirligig. What can I say? The older I get, the more ignorant I become. At times I distrust everything I once thought I knew; the bird is all I have left.

- Leland Bardwell

SHEILA

In her dying she is yet lovely
Her silence swings like a sea-plant
At the ocean's edge; the madonna bones
In their cardboard coloured wrappings
Make no quiver; yes, secret, she lies
And silent.

Ninety years a spinster — they say
She was rich once — nieces and nephews say —
Hay Sheila! One each side of her, solicitors sit
Tearing the hospital cloth
With their ravenous backsides.

Neutered in their defeat,
They have to leave her; her
Silence spreads like the snowberries on her island.
She lifts three fingers like a queen,
Lets time press on the brows of strangers.
She has returned inland to where
The ponies graze. Sheila! The raspberries drip red
A wisp of wind makes the pippins fall.
She runs to her mother's parsley smelling garden
To hear the gladioli stiffen.

LINES FOR MY FATHER

After the furnace had subsided. "Still,
it was a mortal blaze," they said
"Mahogany and sycamore and oak,
The Liffey itself could not have quenched the flames."
Then someone kicked the smouldering remains,
"The fire-brigade was something of a joke."
There was nothing left but fretful wisps of smoke.
He said: "If you do that you'll burn your boots as well."

On the eve of my geography exam
he took me to the Magic Flute
There at the booking office I remonstrated
"I know no geography, I ought to be at home"
"To hell with geography," he stated.

The distant murmur of the waterfall
the salmon's undersides are silver in the sun,
they rest exhausted, then they try again,
the bog-fed Liffey waters push
them back and back. Lax-hlaup. It is suggested
the great scourge Thorkils wandered there
and marvelled at the efforts of the fish.

In Leixlip house the piano stool
stood firm, Victorian and worn,
while outside was Georgian symmetry
of granite, carted stone by stone,
with wicket-keepers broken fingers
he played Leoncavallo, but expertly
I sang (who could hardly be called a singer)
On with the motley ...

PRISON POEM

This way madam! Miss, Mrs, Ms. It's all the same
In the darkened corridor, in the elbow of orange light
Shed by the penitentiary bulb.

She even feels a seam of pity
For the unhappy puzzle of the young cop's face
But she knows she could pedal the flowers of friendship
Till the cows went home and she'd only learn one fact:
He hates her.

For this is the way of things;
Not only is she in the wrong, she is a woman.
The tremble of God's eyelid wouldn't open
Or storm the Bastille of his mind.
How has he sunk so low as to have to walk
With such an evil thing?

Her own identity is something left behind
With generous other days on dirty Dublin streets
Like watching the sad expression on her landlord's face
Or fixing the metre quickly before it's read
Or even a morning queuing for the dole.

But the crash of the heavy lock resounds;
The childhood mortice of an unknown room
And she is again a child on whom fleshless silence
Clamps its morbid teeth.

She lies under the weight of it
In the air that's as cold as salt and with her stare
Breaks up the surface of the cobbled wall
Beneath whose cloak of dust, graffiti, blood,
A million creatures whisper; with or without her
Their parliament is never still.

INISBOFIN

Mikey's eyes see further than the long sea
    in the short bar.
If an island is another land it isn't Ireland
and the islanders' insulated laugh is a valediction
    that no partings fathom.

Yet we return again and again
      as the pleated sea swells
to allow ourselves that moment of joy
as the Melody docks, the crafty old engines
      grinding to a halt
And Mikey's cagey welcome, small drops of merriment
      waltzing in the irises
would make the twelve bens bow down in salutation.

His brother Christy rests athwart the bows
      (he never smiles)
His salt lips are dried by his daily death
      banging from port to port with cargo and caution
His melody is the song he sings when the sun
      dips over the island's spine.

The rest of the crew, Young Jim, in his forty years
      a stranger to both, harbours his eyes
      like the skin of the bog where the sun runs like a
scythe,
languid and orderly in his labour he hurls
      the Guinness kegs on the harbour tip
Short shrift for the returning vagrants
      fron Kensal Rise or Ealing West
or the Johnnie-come-latelies like ourselves
      gratefully settled like plovers on motionless ground
while the crowd disperses and the island, a figure of
eight
      subsides once more in its ocean bed.

Mikey, stately in his sixty years
      drifts to Day's Bar, leaving the future behind him.

FIRST

A dog should die outside, the others said
but I had taken her
scrunched up in my arms,
hidden her in the shed.

We lay together in a shroud of hay
holding death aside
like the curtain in a theatre.
But then it came: the blood.
It spurted from her mouth,
spurted on the flagstones
like a string of beads.

What follows obliterates,
with each new loss,
that accident of grief.
But how can one forget what was one's
first. First anything, first love,
first loss, first kiss.

BREACH BABY

Black panther, he does not
streak through forests.
Back and forth, back and forth
in this house of his.
In this house of his, he paces.

My son who is gone five —
the solitary watcher —
says quietly:

He does not know which way.

He remembers my rib-cage.

CLONDALKIN CONCRETE

Late again! You know we keep regular hours
in Clondalkin Concrete.

I was the Temp.
The one who worked from five past nine till six
with no let up
But they kept regular hours at Clondalkin Concrete

From Clondalkin Concrete I wrote a letter to Paul
I told him I was writing concrete verse
and very soon I would send them, block on block
in Clondalkin Concrete we keep stanzas
numbered and counted carefully, cement and sand
We keep regular poems in Clondalkin Concrete

All the while I worked in Clondalkin Concrete
I must have sold a million tons of blocks
I was a bungalow blitz of a typist
Invoice neat in my work
But I wrote, Dear Paul, I dedicate to you
every block of a concrete stanza
every freezing grain of sand
For I'm up to my neck in Clondalkin Concrete

While directly gazing into my boss's watery studs
All that Fall, I shouted, All that Fall

CHILDREN'S GAMES

Once upon a time
I saw my two children playing
where Karl Marx was lying
with a tombstone on his head;
they were naked from the waist down

and the English around and around said
Better the children dead
than naked from the waist down

Now I was a foreigner
on that cold Highgate Hill
but I bore no ill to the English
no ill

So I toiled away by the Spaniards
where the English were all lovers
and their legs gleamed O
so cold and naked
naked from the waist down

and I tried another graveyard
and found another plot
where Sigmund Freud was lying
in his eiderdown of weeds

My children, I said, romp away
this little strip is yours
for the dead are mostly idle
and do not care if you are naked
naked from the waist down

and the graves began to smile
and the hymn of England fade
and my children took out their pocket knives
and carved on the limey stone:

Dr Freud lies here in the nettles
we are dancing on his head

MEMORY

I remember my mother who hated onions
sex and mongrel dogs,
my father's rusty fingers
wading through butterflies.
So I grew to talk kindly with enemies,
soldiers and policemen.
I stare into the morphine of memory
pressing the needle into the weakest spot.

I wonder does she hold her skirt around her knees
in the heaven she believed in,
the demon sex beaten to a dish-cloth
with semi-colons of thou shalt nots
full stops of self abasement
or does she lie, legs splayed out
for dogs and pictures and others to enter her
face glazed in anticipation
for something she never experienced before.

Last week I visited her grave
a dead wreath had landed askew the weathered cross.
Good day, Ma, I said and lifted the crumbling crown
and hurled it into the fields of Confey.

DOSTOEVSKY'S GRAVE

I am locked in this acropolis
just Feodor and me
I rub my fingers
in his overcoat of stone
gambling my airline ticket
and find in the valley
of my life-line
the gravel of Baden Baden

226

THE PRICE OF SHOES IN RUSSIA

I am an old old woman, *Izvinite*
My fingers are nicotine brown
from endless fags. But I exult
in the wings of the choir
that swing from within
the walls of the cathedral.

Till another old old woman,
older even than I, jumps on me
with the speed of hate
cleaves my head with her umbrella
and calls her grandson to evict me.

Being no fool in my eightieth year
I stuff the burning orb into my pocket
Izvinite I am old and stupid as a dog
I beg forgiveness on my hands and knees.
He tells me his name is Yuri.

Yes I'm Yuri — Yuri from Kharkov
And I'm an ancient Protestant woman
from a Catholic country called Ireland
and I wish I'd never smoked
in the precincts of his church.
Oh Yuri, I cry. But Yuri does not beat me.
He sits me down in the mellow shadow of a tree
near the puddled fish pond in the park
and talks of shoes.

Shoes, he says, lighting up,
are very dear in Kharkov.
I take his *Cosmos* gratefully, inhale and cry
Oh yes, but they are also dear in Dublin
Shoes in Dublin are exceptionally dear.

But socks, he cries, we queue for socks
Not to mention stockings I say.
He is shaken with a fine delight
as we work our way up thighwards
and I burn slowly — from inside with a scorching
love
from my pocket from the burning cigarette
and from the sun above my double vented skull.

When we embrace we agree to meet in Yalta
and feed cyclamen seeds through the eyelids
of Chekov's dacha.

A SINGLE ROSE

I have willed my body to the furthering of science
although I'll not be there
to chronicle my findings
I can imagine all the students
pouring over me
"My God, is that a liver?
and those brown cauliflowers are lungs?"
Yes, sir, a fine example of how not to live.
"And what about the brain?"
"Alas the brain. I doubt if this poor sample
ever had one." As with his forceps
he extracts a single rose.

ROBERT WELCH

Robert Welch was born in Cork city in 1947. He has been
Professor of English at the University of Ulster, Coleraine, since
1984. He has lived and worked in Nigeria, Leeds, West Cork,
and now lives on the north west coast, at Portstewart, with his
wife and four children. His books include a study of nineteenth
century Irish poetry, *Irish Poetry from Moore to Yeats*, a *History of
Verse Translation from the Irish*, and a book on modern Irish
writing, in English and Irish, to be called *Changing States*, due
late 1991. He has edited various collections of essays, including
one on George Moore, and another on *Irish Writers and Religion*;
and has edited a volume in the Penguin Classics series of Yeats's
writings, *W.B.Yeats: Writings on Irish Folklore, Legend and Myth*,
due 1992. He is the editor of the *Oxford Companion to Irish
Literature*, due 1993. He has lectured in France, Germany, Italy,
Holland, Sweden, Austria, Japan, Hungary, Canada, the U S,
and Africa. *Muskerry* is his first collection of poems, published
by The Dedalus Press in 1991

When I was at University of Cork in the '60s I'd walk the four or so miles to the campus (that is on those days that I would turn up for classes). On these walks back and forth, in all weathers, I would hum and sing to myself. Not really to amuse myself, no; more out of panic and anxiety, trying to keep at bay a feeling that not very far below the surface were layers upon layers of contempt, self-hate, anger, futility, and so on, the usual adolescent hormone soup. Sometimes, on these walks, done perhaps seven or eight times a week, I'd lose myself into a kind of trance, improvising on some tune or other, imagining myself a jazz trombonist in Kansas or somewhere, transmitting my full complexity, in ever more beautiful and in tense patterns. Ego, ego, all ego. And yet this longing to transmit, to broadcast the signals of whatever gene-pattern arrived in me and is developing and changing in me, remains. This is why I continue to write despite the futility that always accompanies the beginning to write. It is the hope of rhythm, which is the hope of surprise, the longing for the pattern that is beautiful and inclusive, that is marked by you and no other, the hope for a voice amongst all the other voices, and the belief that there is a value in achieving a voice. I have the sense that the transmission of that rhythm pattern which is yours and no one else's, is prayer; that it is a formal act, that it is lovely; that it is the thing that strikes and moves others, moving them into awareness of new formations.

-*Robert Welch*

THE FEAR ORCHARD

She did not like them, much,
when they were there,
but liked them less
as they were going away.

She reasoned at noon
when the gong was struck for lunch:
"I do not like their pity
nor my own expectation.

"I shall write biographies of the unborn,
and watch their lives
collide with fact
and show how gradually they tire."

Once there had been a voice
saying she could not be distracted,
but it was long ago,
and had she heard correctly?

Fear was now relentless
and fierce: a steel triangle
hanging in an orchard
glinting in blue smoke.

THE MARIE CELINE

Sucking at her nipple
he soothes her blood.
His pull comforts
her bones and the
slack skin in folds
across her stomach.

Somewhere a door
slams in the white
corridor. Quiet deepens.
His eyes open: slits
of pure blue as he drives
his mouth into her soft flesh.

On all fours in the nursing
ward a cleaner scrubs
terracotta tiles. The brush
sloshes easily through
thickening foam. Her grimed
hand is beautiful.

THE 'PAV': 1967

Saturday evenings in the Pavilion
Restaurant. Dinner at 8.00 p.m.
We'd still be quiet from the peace
of being together since 6.00 o'clock.
Evening now really settling in. The long
Cork evenings, with the air stilled,
even though this was the main street
we were looking down upon. Huge red
curtains swept up from the crimson
carpet; across the dining room,
a coal fire burned, though not because
of cold. This would be October,
maybe, with our lives before us,
a winter of maturity ahead
bestowing now, upon our silence,
a gravity of joy and tenderness.
There is fear and there is failure,
and there is hope, too;
not much else to say of those quiet
evenings, full of darkening light,
that would not be intrusion.

MEMOIRS OF A KERRY PARSON

I

In the evenings I would fumble in my loneliness,
colliding with the furniture
in the darkened parlour.

Sometimes I would try
to character the past,
but never got beyond the opening lines:

The Bishop of Limerick thought the spires of Protestant
churches would civilize the County of Kerry. That
severe elegance, he thought, would serve to...

Always the continuing end.
My tongue would arch for speech,
but readiness would dissolve
in contemplation of a lichen stain
on the greyness of my boundary wall.

II

Her face that evening at my leaded panes.
Did her skin derive its texture
from the grey stone walls, the lichen stains?

When she turned aside to face the setting sun
her auburn hair fell back
to show the lovebites on her neck.

I closed my eyes, appalled,
and when I opened them again
the diamond panes were clear.

III

Green lichen marks the flagstone
covering my grave.
No bells can ring
where I sleep through the fen.

There are two who keep me company:
a red-haired girl to irk the shadow
at my door; and a bearded man who brings
news of politics and kings.

The girl stands in her shadow, hoping I may come,
being now no more
than waiting's phantom,
her cold in the northward facing stone.

The bearded man is kind.
His reddish hair enhances fresh and mottled skin;
a starched and snow-white ruff
upholds his courtier's head.

He turns to me to talk
but his voice is slowed down
to stress each word as if
it were a thread unpicked

from a tapestry of the possible,
the picker knowing he has the skill
to weave another set of chance
from the gathering riot of thread:

See that what you do
conforms to what occurs,
even as the tree bole stirs
to take upon itself a self that's new.

IV

The pale yellow of the primrose
thaws the dark green of the Spring.

Colours then go deepening, deepening,
until the small space of my grave
cannot hold me any more.

Come and search my tomb.

You will find that I have gone.

V

I am going the hundred yards
or so to Kilmalkedar church, its arch
a tension of the slotted years
in the lives of my parishioners.

The last one died
when I was twenty two,
a new recruit from Trinity College,
polished buckles on my shoes.

From behind the hedgerows
Catholic girls would peep. I could never tell
their faces from the flowers
they were always laughing through.

Now their tiny faces
crowd inside the pendant crowns
of the crimson fuchsia flowers.
In the autumn they are blood upon the road.

VI

Eventually I shall have been
a chink of daylight in a drystone wall;
a crevice in a rock;
mere weathering on
the grey stone of Kilmalkedar's arch.

And shall have been again
what I once became.

UPPER EVERGREEN ROAD

Two streets met, at an angle of thirty degrees:
across the road a public house, tied
to Beamish's brewery; to the left
a limestone wall, settled, cool
and untroubled. On the corner
opposite the pub there was the potato store.
Spuds in jute sacks, with the nap
turned down, smelt of Nohoval,
Ballycotton, Youghal. Even here,
in the city, the faint tang of seaweed
which manured the crop. Right,
a little way up the street, a tiny shop
where the cobbler sat. When you came in
he looked up, his lips crammed with iron.

OVER AND OVER

Sombre now in Stratford the rain falls
and it has been so for such a vain
long time. The gravediggers come into
the yard, where grows a mulberry tree.

236

Each time it takes them longer to do
what they do each time they come.
They are burying the same man
over and over and over again.

Somewhere back along the lanes, beneath
a creaking sign, an old herbalist sits,
studying the garden designs of the past
and of the future. He sits on, waiting.

Upstairs, a woman rests her hand
against the oak of a desk and breathes.
Breathing the aroma of the forest
where it grew, she is thinking of the man

who's buried now beneath the mulberry.
Years ago he planted it, before he left
the town, to come back and be buried
beneath its canopy and fruited shade.

They keep on laying him down, and
again they come back into the yard
carrying him; there are only two of them
and no-one else, to bear the heavy oak.

NOVEMBER '89 : PRAGUE

It was an anxious time, in the room
behind the balcony that overlooked the square.
All the newsmen, all the media persons
were told, in rage, to leave, then,
abruptly, we were asked to stay.
It was worrying to be selected.

We knew the stories behind the stories,
or at least knew enough of them
to know that the popular uprising
was being managed; to what extent
no-one could say, not even those
who had arranged for the trampling
of one of the local agitators in the square,
the release of news of his death,
but under a different name. And all this
with the help of the security forces,
intent in undermining the old regime,
to bring in "new blood"; that was the
phrase they used, "new blood".
Events now in this room of shouting faces,
livid with exhaustion, in a fug of smoke
were moving to the climax: the big conclusion.
The work had gone on for months, mostly
in silence, in the exchanges of understanding
thsoe who ache for power only know.
He came in, dishevelled and tired,
a man out of time, almost out of energy,
and spoke off the balcony to the vast sea
of upturned faces. No barking or sorrow;
hesitancy, caution were his mood and attitude.
After the first, searching, sentences the crowd
grew intensely quiet, expectant, waiting;
the square became a space of dark silence,
as he spoke into the night air
his weariness, his qualifications, his effort
at what might begin to be called, once more,
with every awareness of the caution needed,
freedom.

AUGUST '91 : MOSCOW

At an angle of forty five degrees
the statue of the founder
of the KGB is lifted from the plinth,
two great cranes having been
brought into the square for the purpose.
The almost saintly face, the heavy coat,
the calm reassuring set of the lips
look kindly from this angle,
vulnerable even, tender. Shouts of rage
and enthusiasm go up, as the hawsers
strain, grip, swing slightly.
Up in the cabins, with the levers,
the drivers haul and pull, balancing.
In the dark they cannot see
each others' faces, but they know,
in the heft and tug, the shudder
in the levers, which way to slacken, give, or pull,
how to accommodate the moving mass of bronze.
The saintly face looms into the light an instant,
then back out again, into the dark.

IACHALL

The empty bag light in my fingers,
swirled round a complete circle, touching
the dusty pavement at the lowest point.
First the totally bald butcher, Mr. Long,
who'd cut the chops, slicing down
to the bone, then the prising each one apart,
to get the hacksaw in, ripping
through to the scrubbed deal beneath.
Then liver, nicely cut, his thick fingers
gently pulsing the slab of meat to the knife's keen edge.

Miss O'Riordan next, the tang of salt
and bacon and of sawdust. A dark shop
with hands, flitches, still in muslin,
hung from the iron bar across the ceiling.
On the marble shelf were lined up
the cheaper cuts: smoked streaky,
loose thin sausages, white puddings, scraps.
The prize was a pound of bits for one and six
Back up Summerhill, the convent above,
then home to the emptying out of the shopping bag,
and praise, and liver and bacon for the tea.

(Iachall - Irish for "handle" or "duty")

PAUL MURRAY

Paul Murray was born in Newcastle, County Down, in 1947, and educated at St Malachy's College, Belfast. In 1966 he entered the Dominican Order. He teaches at the Dominican Studium in Tallaght in Dublin, at University College, Dublin, and in Rome at the Angelicum University. His publications include three books of poetry, *Ritual Poems*, New Writers' Press 1971, *Rites and Meditations*, The Dolmen Press 1982, and in 1991 The Dedalus Press published his collection of poems, *The Absent Fountain*. His other books are *The Mysticism Debate*, Herald Press USA 1977, and *T.S.Eliot and Mysticism*, Macmillan 1991.

"The Art of Poetry", which is offered here by way of introduction, gives expression to one of the more paradoxical and humbling experiences of writing, namely that the process of discovering one's own voice somehow initiates one into an awareness of the many voices and strands of tradition to which one is heir. Of the poems which follow, "Introit" and "Meditation III" are from *Rites and Meditations*. The remaining poems, including "The Art of Poetry", are from *The Absent Fountain*.

THE ART OF POETRY

I

Say what you will,
though the desire seem crazy,
the gift is not distinct
from the desire,
and you must try
to shape out of their cloth
a timeless, woven music.
And even if the strands
of thought,
the threads of imagery you use,
have with rare love and ease
by other hands been drawn,
today, it is your weave,
your love, these threads obey
— though still
through time unravelling.

II

As the slow wheel of language turns
and as the brilliant loom
of thought and of emotion changes,
gradually, slowly,
these newly-borrowed images and forms,
these stolen traces,
these hooked, half-conscious memories
of theme and phrase, are now
being drawn into the very warp and woof,
woven into the cadence
of your own heart's music.

- Paul Murray

INTROIT

This morning,
on entering the cold chapel,

    I looked first
to the sun, as the pagan does,
not by strict custom
nor by constraint, but because

    I too, as creature,
sense man's primitive emotion:
his need to praise.
And so, like priest or pagan,

    according
as the sun moves, I perform
this ancient ritual.
And though not always able

    to approach,
often, effaced in light, I stand
before this
chalice of the morning.

    I break this
ordinary bread as something holy.

from MEDITATIONS

III

With those friends who disclaim all knowledge
of God, I boast and I say,
    "I know Him",
and I say I am speaking from my own experience.

But my friends say: "Be reasonable, how
can you know Him, how can you be so sure
that you are not self-deceived?" This question,
I know, is honest; and I know it demands
for an answer not these obscure words
about experience, but the clear evidence
of a man's life. However, I will say it
here again, and even to my own doubting heart,
and to my five agnostic senses: "I know Him".

THE ABSENT FOUNTAIN

"To him who is dying of thirst the absent fountain,
for all its absence, is nevertheless sweeter than
were a world in which there were no fountains"
                              - Antoine de Saint-Exupéry

My soul
was dry, and dry
as dust
lay the roots
of my awareness.

I had almost
forgotten you were alive.

But like
the sea-spray
or like the rising
spray
of a fountain

your absence
grazed my lips
and left its freshness
falling
through the air.

"KNOW THYSELF"

There is a world within you
    no one has ever seen,
a voice no one has ever heard,
    not even you.
As yet unknown
    you are your own seer,
your own interpreter.
    And so, with eyes and ears
grown sharp for voice or sign,
    listen well —
not to these words
    but to that inward voice,
that impulse beating in your heart
    like a far wave.
Turn to that source, and you
    will find
what no one has ever found,
    a ground within you
no one has ever seen,
    a world beyond the limits
of your dream's horizon.

THE BIRD MAN

Homage to Sweeney Astray

Pity the mad poet
— never —
he will despise your pity.

But rather
envy him his madness:

he who has climbed
like a stray thrush
far into the sky

who has brushed with his wings
yet caught
in his hand like a sword

the white pain
arrows of white stars
forked lightning.

THRESHOLD

Not at the pointed
hour of ecstasy
nor at the furthest edge
of being,
but here, in the even
close-knit hours
among the weekday
goings-on
of wind and weather,
here is our hidden threshold
of perception,
here we must wait
until the doors of the present
swing open
on new hinges.

THE CRY

When I awoke, the room was dark
  and the rain was beating
against the window pane.
  It was the room that faces out to sea,
the room in which I was born.

And from my bed I thought I saw
  the dark curtains lifting
and moving, and thought I heard
  far out to sea
a lone seabird crying in the storm.

But, as I listened, there leaned
  against my heart
— and it made me tremble — the memory
  of that other dream,
the same dream, that other night.

And I thought to myself: Is it
  possible, then,
I am not awake at all, and the rain
  is not now beating
against the window pane.

And there is no seabird crying
  in the storm,
but that, instead, once more,
  this stark
isolated cry is, perhaps, my own?

THE DISTANT PIER

How it is that words then said
and silences we kept
on that occasion have given
shape and meaning to my solitude
I cannot explain.

It was late in the afternoon,
I remember,
and we were walking at our ease
back and forth
on the grey, granite pier
near Ostia Antica,
with then, as now, only
the sound of your words
— not the shape, not the meaning —
distinct in my ear.

But those words, your words,
remain like music in my solitude,
and the sound of your voice
is like clear water lapping
and breaking
against the prow of my mind.

LIGHTNING

In the fissure of the moment,
in the sudden lightning
of God's mercy

the saint
is indistinguishable
from the sinner,

and the flowers of earth
and the flowers of heaven
are the same.

HOMAGE TO THE VOID

The first glimpse
of you — I remember —
was of something perilous
yet lovely.
You were like a source
that had no beginning,
like a spring welling up
in the eyes of oblivion.
And so perilous you seemed
and so intolerably lovely
I thought to myself:
"It is a dream
it is no more than that".

But what a weight of absence
— O Nameless One —
as you leaned against me
suddenly
like a wall of air,
as you stared into my eyes
and stared through me,
your eyes and gaze
incurious
yet all-perceiving,
your dark eyes
like the closed wings
of a dreaming butterfly.

THE UNMANIFEST

Obscure and dark
as ever, yet
leaving, as it does,
every form
every gesture shining
as it passes,
I had thought
the illumination
of our time
would make it visible.

But it is plain sense
to me now
that, immanent
though it is
and radiant,
this ray
of darkness,
this torch of the void
cannot be proven
nor yet disproven.

PHOENIX

It is within these eyes
(O cruel blindness!
O burning nest of mirrors!)
it is within these eyes:
what the self cannot know
what the far crest of being cannot see
when it stops
when it turns back
and looks at itself.

It is within these eyes
(O pupil of unawareness!
O gaze of absence!)
that the scorched, imperishable
wings of the phoenix
are opening, and the freed void
rises above a blaze of suns
and death
burns into silence.

THE FABLE OF BEING

I have heard it again
echoing and singing
out of nowhere

that small
hum-note
calling and calling

like an ancient hymn.

*

"Come", it sings,
and the echo
of its voice in my ear
sings: "Come,
whoever you are. See
where creation's weights
and wheels are held.
Come now to where
each sliding hour,
each form
recalls its silent origin.
Here where you stand
the youngest light
and the oldest darkness
are beginning to mingle."

*

When I looked, I saw
rising
above the waters of the void
a star of the impossible.

And in my eyes it shone
and in my soul
like the appearance of Now
like the existence of Yes.

ON LIVING LIFE TO THE FULL

When your heart is empty
and your hands are empty

you can take into your hands
the gift of the present

you can experience in your heart
the moment in its fullness.

*

And this you will know,
though perhaps you may not yet
understand it,

this you will know:

that nothing
of all you have longed for
or have sought to hold fast
can relieve you of your thirst,
your loneliness,

until you learn
to take in your hands
and raise to your lips
this cup of solitude
this chalice of the void

and drain it to the dregs.

BRIAN COFFEY

Brian Coffey was born in Dublin in 1905. He taught in America and in London and is living in retirement in Southampton. He has published many collections of poetry and translations. In 1934 Samuel Beckett named him, with Denis Devlin, as "without question the most interesting of the youngest generation of Irish poets." In 1991 Brian Coffey returned to Dublin for the launch of "Poems and Versions: 1929-1990", published by The Dedalus Press.

ABOUT POETRY

Those who write verse today have often to attempt answers to the question: What is poetry? Not easy to do, off the cuff. One is reduced to quoting from others, among whom the philosopher Jacques Maritain, whose "Creative Intuition in Art and Poetry", (Pantheon Books, New York 1953) covers this area and from which I select the following short passage:

"Modern poetry cannot be judged and understood in the perspective of classical aesthetics and mere literature. We might as well ask a butterfly-hunter to catch an octopus or a whale. In the seemingly purely verbal researches of a Mallarmé or a Valéry, a crucial spiritual experience and the consciousness of a tragic struggle were involved. Nothing is more significant in this regard than the letter in which Mallarmé tells his friend Cazalis of his struggle with God: *'ma lutte terrible avec ce vieux et méchant plumage, terrassé heureusement, Dieu!'* 'I fell, victorious', he goes on to say. 'I am now impersonal, and no longer Stephan, whom you knew - but an aptitude which the spiritual universe possesses to see itself and to develop, through that which was me' - *'à travers ce qui fut moi.'* As a result he is perfectly dead, *'je suis parfaitement mort.'* And he will give expression to the Universe in three poems in verse 'of a purity that man has not reached', and in 'four poems in prose, on the spiritual conception of Nothingness.' And as for Paul Valéry, it is enough to read his last book, *Mon Faust*, to realize the seriousness of the spiritual struggle of a man who all his life endeavoured to be more intelligent than both Faust and Mephistopheles. With Mallarmé and Valéry, the option for the rejection of transcendence taught modern poetry the experience of the void (and also, as concerns Mallarmé, a faint hope in magic.) I wonder whether the Olympus of words to whose mysterious rites the great mind of Joyce dedicated itself did not emerge from some similar experience of the void — and a haunting memory of a lost paradise guarded by the sword of a fiery Irish angel."

Maritain does not refer, in that context, to other poets who either have faced the void or have chosen otherwise. One supposes that Samuel Beckett, Robert Graves, Laura Riding and Yosip Mandelstam should be studied more deeply from this aspect.

As regards that vast crowd of the second or third order, who churn out an unending flow of songs and verse, I put forward a short passage from a poem of my own (which tells the story of Topman Ti — who sought political mastery and failed, and which deals with the education of poets:

> True platonist Ti'd fix the poets
> of whom his Toppers had found an itch
> in each conurb of the square coast
> Poor lot peepers to a man/miss
> casing each other vetting muses
> solo here threesome there
> boyboy here girlgirl there
> with an H here and a C there
> here acid there grass
> everywhere a touch of speed .
> everyone committed
> how they were committed
> outside Plato's farm
> "Dese guys jes' want novelty"

swore Ti "but not in Topos no sir"
He activated MANIAC
asked for a name and got it
Angus MacSorass of That Ilk
Here was a bard knew no silk
on his muscular thighs
just breeze through the hair under kilt
This copious bard was just coping
with keeping alive on no fame
when he saw poet Jon on the job
with a girl on the beach
lush the girl peach her bloom
on the tide "Jon Jon"
howled MacSorass "Jon
get your best jeans back on
for shame" Then Topman came on
MacSorass he dubbed Top Poet
of United Toposian Arts
Assigned him ten Toppers to purge with
using nine grams per head
of second best shaped lead
MacSorass to bellow the slogan
"Self to itself is the Same
Novelty Fiction Supreme"

Nine A.M. on Re-Ed Day
cracked bell to toll the dirge
Top Speakers all at wattage max
MacSorass juicing up the tracks
"Poets" he howled "do ye hear me
do ye want that ba' in the heid
Poets unite Poets Quick March
off to the saltmines Left Right Left
"Poets Get on wi your arrrt"

And, to finish on a different note, a short passage from
my own poem "Advent":

"Into this world I came well-knowing
my own do follow me against the lethal odds
My broken body veils what saves and salves
Wear my pierced skin   agonise
in my night which confounds untruth"

Must it be this way

How would one better have had it done

- Brian Coffey

*** ___ ***

THE TIME THE PLACE

Motionless silence
To be remembered
when brighter flowers fade
in later sunsets

That once when waves
at full tide stayed and sun
slant lighted expectant
content and sure who waited

and vainly for who
without appointment yet defaulted
All wanting fruit of other's will
is wanting sadly sadly wanting

Did Menelaus see Helen fail
follow her flight in mind's eye
or a Joan check by mere advertence
Darby's pale infidelities

Prone I stared at the night sky
quite recognizably starred
knew as little as he or she
how another mewards fared

LEADER

The dream revisited
thirty years on
held whitewashed cave
good books the handfull
pale light of candle sole
murmur of camp and arms
all hearts' warmth
flowing round leader
at search for newest
beautifulest words

He was to say
"My people are poor and blank
like clean paper
take the imprint I choose
in the world within
the world without

I am their sun their source
father mother
all their ancestors
all their futures"

Truthless poor
people and leader

"And
what had they had before
Little or nothing but walls
thin bodies empty minds
Enough was to huddle
at night by pairs
ready for rousing"

What had they had from him
Pain and death
by one and one and one

that People might live for ever
history no river banked
beneath placid suns
beyond gorge and rapids
nor someday rest from strife

What he had known was rapids
Could rapids be for ever
Rapids would be for ever
for unborn armies drowning
living the pure concern with death
the newest word *Revolt*
the beautifulest word *Unending*
branding the people with
Stasis For Ever Barricades

Yet what do the Wanderers tell us
That it moves still   It moves

Truly
there it was
behind thirty years
the rickety chair
and the ghost
experience unwraps
in leader
in the revisited room

POEM

To sleep sometimes I dream
I mean that wild surmise
in curtains parting where rise
the sleeping to what does seem

in frames of random shift
taste of aloe on tongue
smoke of dailiness in lung
gleam hopeless of vague drift

when at last ground rules
of Kickpawkissmaw verity
or changing psych of levity
in types archont-or-on-gules

open if that is how it is
the introverted dormant eye
to what daylight dare not try
the thin ice the near miss

LIMINAL

He does not ask
she does not ask
whose eyes hold whose
in perfect light

Light for light lost
in lost eyes light
in green spires crossed
by sapphire blades

Silence on broken wings
in light so clear
retractile fear
defeating

Did he ask
did she ask
did each ask other why
green knives cleave blue planes
blue flames fire green thorns
should either say

Secret sustained
reigns secreted

When he lifts gold spears
when she spreads rose leaves
he knows her need
she his and

patient hands compose
the white the fruitful tide

ELEISON II

Watch the runi-builders working
guess and choose and guess again
make laws by teams
for the likes of us
chew the fly-blown rag
of general good
aping the old style

Then the tied cord
threaded through pierced feet
foiled escape on bare hill
from hot or cold
wild dog or snake
yet the doing they hid
for shame was it

Where sun has shone
time and time again
uncountable
held back till dark
to send the wrapped flesh
seawards unseen unmourned

See now see
millions strong they are
who millions have undone
since dawn
their haunted eyes
emptied of love
kind trusting love
plead necessity
bitter the cruel times
the lying rulers

Below the stairs
ergot it was
emptied with the slops
or kick in the belly
like owing the cat
always a way
kill on arrival
for the unwanted
or smiling farmyard witch
or backstreet knitter

But now it's welfare
clean white tiles
skilled aseptic hands
we do a legal job
from scrape to disposal
saved from bastards
by flame that roars louder
than any baby scream

PAINTERLY

Remembering Chagall
Always what charms is a garden

Evening slight moon she
without whom pain and loss

Nicotiana open where
he has been drawn to
to see her open eyes
silence then deep eyes
silence hers silence his

She was he saw a woman
fit to bear a child
Her deft hands would make bread
her place entire she would care over
nor ever would loose his care
to keep her self selfsame
secret living veiled

He knew him hers on sight
through that scented place
while moon slight moon
supplied for the fading light

For him it had happened early
How fortunate a man
how magical he would make his world
for her in paint and show
bird pull a sleigh
of happy souls to happy goals
o lively bird o teeming scene
and show men dance on roofs and there
a crooked ass stare out the sun
spinning below a hill

Green and red and blue known
only to him who mixed them
yellow yellow colour of love
gliding figures wings in air
dawns red nocturnes green
woman centre point
man always with her

So it was so it was
they swore their troth
they shared a life
and death did them part

Now memory worked instead of sight
gave silence distance a quiet space
in farview imaged her remote
other gone herwards far a star

By desire his will could move
where once the sight of her was spur
and source and nourishment and goal
and by desire he shared our pain
shouldered crosses increased us all

so that we love her blue face
at rest in comet whose face is green
while Gavin fiddling on a cloud
with jumping cows and piping clowns
and roofs with grazing horses on
and kinds of birds at birdlike play
invite us into that painted sway
of colour veiled like her heart

Maybe within an eternity
he might tell the tale
what his woman is not was

How could she not for ever be
how not indeed

CAVE

Woman body that tender is
beyond conceit
implies no prudery on woman's part
enjoins on man a role of worshipping
patient of change   a waiting on moments hers
lest he force pattern on response
to unasked questions
blur sudden answering   him left witless
                        all or nothing due

Do not wonder or look askance
when he explores a world of absence
finds geographies of pure reminding
what eyes have seen what ears have heard
what every sensing offers him of her
outside   inside
and names hills valleys depths folds
to image her   all inadequate

The tale is sad   seldom all told
Were one to enter   find at highest dark her words
  "Come this far in and find me not
   Even joying I am still to find"
what a fall it would be
what loss of open land untramelled
not to follow

Try it as you will
secret reigns secreted and source
of quest   hope and all

"She" he says and not define
nor circumscribe and yet abide
not in ignorance

Where false words rule
union disunites unwary pairs
turning up shapeless to the scene

She must not lose herself in him
he must not lose himself in her
Clouds race through clouds like meeting galaxies
No union there   part excluding part
What loving is not

In the true world where none are gods
two may become one heart
not wreck each other
how and whence and whither the cruel tale

Just beginning often pain enough
to foreclose futures
in fancied exhaustive loving out
to death in darkness
all hope spent

BELLA

Silent the woman in her chair
hands at rest whose eyes send back
in-going light to eyes outside

The painter takes the dark-dyed light
fortunate working how he sees
what that woman kept in her heart

visions — search as he might — not grasped
while days count down for her
her blood drop by drop

one-for-one   her people killed one by one
to sate a vacuous monster-horde
moving in her view

as move the Dvina deeps
"That I would write" she said
finding again an ancient style

on papers dropped around her house
"That you may read when I have gone"

"My papers"
                    Her last words

THOMAS McCARTHY

Thomas McCarthy was born in Co. Waterford in 1954 and educated at University College, Cork. In 1977 he won the Patrick Kavanagh award. In 1978-9 he was a member of the International Writing Program at the University of Iowa. In 1984 he received the American-Irish Foundation's literary award. He has published, in 1978 *The First Convention*, (Dolmen Press), in 1981 *The Sorrow Garden* (Anvil Press), 1984 *The Non-Aligned Storyteller*, (Anvil Press) and in 1989 *Seven Winters in Paris* (Anvil/Dedalus Press).

One can find all kinds of excuses for writing poems. By the time a writer is an adult it is a compulsive activity; it is no longer linked to the trauma that hurt one into verse. Poems cannot be explained by reference to personal material, but their creation does fill a void. For a poet the poems become a strong link with experience, they confirm experience in some strange way; they are part of "the prodigious search of appearances" created by the trained technical eye. The poet's temperament is the eye through which things become seen. I am sure that part of the reward of writing is to see things confirmed in the way that one's needs require that they be confirmed. That is also part of the intelligent reader's reward. It is an event both aesthetic and psychiatric.

It is difficult, indeed fatal, to propose an aesthetic of poetry. Theories of poetry are part of the tyranny of metaphysics. What is good or bad for poetry is not a metaphysical question: in truth, one cannot generalise away from the experience of reading a poem. Anymore than one can write poems based on general principles. Every poem that gets written is a victory over general principles and theories of poetry. A poem is a personal event. This is what distinguishes it from an academic principle of criticism, for example, or from a political ideology. I have always been interested in politics, but politics as daffodils or bogs or working-class suburbs. It is important for me to say this. I am clear about the use of politics; I am aware that poetry is the very antithesis to politics. What a poet creates is a personal voice.

I am also aware that I use my father a lot. But I use at least three fathers, none of whom are my real father. They are the fathers of each poem's need. The father of the Party is not my dead father in *The Sorrow Garden*; the father of "The First Convention" is not the father of "Counting the Dead on the Radio". Sometimes when I address a father I am talking to my former self, to a self that had certain political beliefs. In poems that address the Dail, for instnce, in *Seven Winters in Paris*, I use the father image because a father-son relationship best describes the intimacy and shared guilt that I feel with the past.

At the moment I am trying to write poems that address my real father, Paddy McCarthy of Cappoquin in

Co. Waterford. He is the lost father of *The Sorrow Garden*.
It is important to state that each poem well written is a
great joy, a technical, professional joy that an athlete or
a sculptor has. And each good poem retains that core of
well-being despite the mawkishness or horror of the
theme. In a world where belief is fragmentary, where
millenial systems collapse in days, the poems over time
accumulate into quite an adequate epistemology.

- Thomas McCarthy

***

STATE FUNERAL

"Parnell will never come again, he said. He's there,
all that was mortal of him. Peace to his ashes."
James Joyce, *Ulysses*

That August afternoon the family
Gathered. There was a native *deja-vu*
Of Funeral when we settled against the couch
On our sunburnt knees. We gripped mugs of tea
Tightly and soaked the TV spectacle;
The boxed ritual in our living-room.

My father recited prayers of memory,
Of monster meetings, blazing tar-barrels
Planted outside Free-State homes, the Broy-
Harriers pushing through a crowd, Blueshirts;
And, after the war, De Valera's words
Making Churchill's imperial palette blur.

269

What I remember is one decade of darkness,
A mind-stifling boredom; long summers
For blackberry picking and churning cream,
Winters for saving timber or setting lines
And snares: none of the joys of here and now
With its instant jam, instant heat and cream:

It was a landscape for old men. Today
They lowered the tallest one, tidied him
Away while his people watched quietly.
In the end he had retreated to the first dream,
Caning truth. I think of his austere grandeur;
Taut sadness, like old heroes he had imagined.

THE SORROW GARDEN

1 HOLE, SNOW

It is an image of irreversible loss,
This hole in my father's grave that needs
Continuous filling. Monthly now, my
Uncle comes to shovel a heap of earth
From the spare mound. Tear-filled, he
Compensates the collapse of his brother's
Frame. I arrive on my motor-bike to help
But he will not share the weight of grief.

It is six months since my father's death
And he has had to endure a deep snow;
All night it came down, silently like time,
Smoothing everything into sameness. I
Visited the winter-cold grave, expecting
A set of his footprints, a snow-miracle.

2 SMALL BIRDS, VOICES

These are the neatly twisted sounds of death,
Those small brown birds singing, small winter
Birds clinging to an overhanging bough.
Never in life did I know him to stare
So silence-stricken for one brief moment.

These birds recall the voices of his life:
A low cold note is the voice of torment
From childhood poverty and the brief, light
Notes are the tones of Love and Marriage.

"There's the beginning of *your* life's troubles",
A neighbour said at his grave. I arranged
The wilting wreath-flowers, feigning numbness.
Something, perhaps his voice, told me even then
How much of Love, Sorrow, Love one life contains.

3 MISTING-OVER

These bright evenings I ride
through the young plantation
by the river; at times I can
see the young trees clearly
through the collapsing mist.

Sometimes in the misted river
at dusk his face at my left
shoulder has become distinctly
settled and lined with peace.

271

But now in the clouded pools
I drive through on the avenue,
he no longer calls out as if
injured by my rear wheel, but
is happy as clay, roads, memory.

4 LOST WORDS, SORROWS

It's difficult to believe that it could
go on; this wanting to participate
in a rigid plan of water and wood,
words and wood and other inanimate
worlds that cannot explain sorrow.

Around me I find the forms that know
his lack of living. The wooden sculpture
on a shelf points to its lack of finish,
calls for a finishing touch, for his sure
and solid polish. I pray for its wish.

As if water could explain my crying,
I visited the salmon-weir after
a snow-fall. The fish were manoeuvring
through the spray, determined to get over
protective obstacles of wood and stone.

Like salmon through water, like virgin wood
disturbed into its form in art, his death
obfuscates words irrecoverably. Death plays
its own tune of vision and shadow. It has
attached itself as a vocabulary of change.

THE PHENOMENOLOGY OF STONES

for Catherine

These summer days I carry images of stone,
Small pebbles from a photographer's shelf
Made smooth by a million years of sea and salt.
Sunlight shines roundly into their small room,
Twisting black grains into crystals and gems:
Lights call like young birds from their surfaces,
Sparrows of light flying from graves, from places
Where the dead had grown; the sorrow-gardens.

But the silence of stone quietens the mind
And calms the eye. Like their girl-collector —
In her deep solitude the stones are moved.
She is their dream-collector, pouring her kind-
ness into their sleeping form. They gather
Fables about themselves to entertain such love.

THE PRESIDENT'S MEN

There's dust on Mr Dineen's boots! Where has
he been canvassing, I wonder? What house
has unlatched a half-day of harvest work
to listen to his talk? My father knows
the Party poll, the roll-calls of promise;
the roads we shall take when I am older
in search of power. We'll find it like cress
on farms of green and vegetal water.

The sound of bagpipe music! Just listen!
From my father's shoulder I can see above
the crowd, Mr Dineen's careful parade,
men struggling to keep the roadway open,
sunlight in my father's hair, the glitter of
pipers' braids; the President's cavalcade.

QUESTION TIME

Question time at the end of another Election Year;
Senators and their wives dancing on the ballroom floor;
children in corners dropping crisps and cream,
their fathers ordering them home, their mothers in crinoline
having to put them outside to sulk in the Christmas dark.
Enmities dissolving now in a sea of drink and smoke and talk.

Who was Robert Emmet's mistress? Who was Kitty O'Shea?
Which I.R.A. man was shot on his own wedding-day?
How many death-warrants did Kevin O'Higgins sign?
So much to answer between the buffet meal and wine —
But the prize is a week in Brussels, money for two,
and kisses from two Euro-M.P.s just passing through.

THINKING OF MY FATHER IN THE MUSÉE PICASSO

It breaks my heart to think of your failures,
for you were not a bad man, just hopeless.
The lost Party, those lethal social forces
that broke your will broke others less poor.
Talent is a muscle that needs constant exercise
and Ireland was your disagreeable milieu —
all the end-of-term banter of the Dail
couldn't hide that truth. But look at Picasso:
he was a bullish, besieged Stalinist,
yet he worked and worked and worked.
Every butterfly of an idea he embraced became art;
and every false move he made used material
more permanent and beautiful than the Dail.

from SEVEN WINTERS IN PARIS

XXII

The Luxembourg Gardens. A school of chairs
sitting empty, awaiting *Herald Tribune* or *Le Monde*.
A busker makes a hundred notes on solitude.

XXIII

Dead for France, dead for Liberation —
a pock-mark, two pock-marks, near
St Germain-des-Prés:
the splintered cheek-bones of Christ.

XXIV

The Latin Quarter. You are my Héloïse;
only time will tell if I lose my marbles.

XXV

The bicycles speed past Picasso's studio:
horses on their way, pedalling, to see
the thoroughbreds of M. Delacroix.

XXVI

I beat a retreat from St.-John Perse;
his first editions beyond our reach —
sycamore leaves litter the shop-front
like tunic fragments at Austerlitz.

AUSTRALIA

Wool falls like a tumbling kitten.
You finish the last row, frantic with exile,
and tack the sides of a child's blue jumper.
Sheets are folded. A king-size tablecloth

of stiff damask is wrapped in tissue.
You fold the clothes of your unborn children,
without sentiment but fiercely private.
The pride in your fingers is detailed.

Australia has caught in your throat like fever,
love-fever, something from childhood.
The removal men have compressed your adult life
into cubic yards. If Australia could

only see you now, full of a cracked desire,
it would split its reefs with welcome.
Oz is the father you've been waiting for
— QUANTAS the wild lover and groom.

ISLAND OF IDLENESS

I push from the shore of our nightly bed,
brittle with sleep, naomhog at Dunquin.
East wind of a sleepless night stings my eyes.
I shelter from the squalls of parenthood.
Fog clings to the bedroom window. A child cries.

Boats lie scattered on the rocks —
one or two great wrecks, the M.V.Freud,
the L.E.Dr.Spock, are water-loosened,
cut down to a land-locked keel;
to so much crusting oxide of the heart.

We're gathered up into the morning's swell.
Water slops and sprays against the gunwales.
I recall again that the sea is an horrific fear,
green with depth, sick with power.
We ride the crests of the parenting day,

Blasket Sound of wails and griefs,
bail as hard as we can, against time,
love against the current, warmth against spray.
The sea and its cargo of beliefs
falls against us in a wall of brine.

Think again of the coves we delighted in,
deep starchy beaches of conversation,
the year 1982, a place to watch the western sun;
private island of exhausted passion.

Others called plaintively from their parent-boats
while we heard the wind, whistling sexual
innuendos through the tide. Stones at Coominole
hardly dreamed as fully. Your sleeping mouth
I kissed again, again your nakedness —
pleasure of adult love, island of idleness

NORTH HARBOUR, CAPE CLEAR

The Naomh Ciaran resting in its pocket of water,
children throwing bottles
into the pub incinerator —
pop goes Halloween:
the conversations of the day become vapour,

277

how thin the Taoiseach looked
after his stay in hospital, how full
the island is for the weekend;
like a beached whale bulging at the fins.

A pint of Heineken is being pulled
in Cotters' or Burkes' or at the Club;
as eagerly awaited as a registered letter
from Munich or San Francisco —
For our children remember us.
For you cannot get an island out of your head,
but carry it forever, painful, luminous:
a ferry-boat waiting at the harbour mouth.